To Deirdre

Life goals, g...

Happy Mothers Day 2020

Love you AOA!————→

Momma

A

MORE

Beautiful

LIFE

A MORE *Beautiful* LIFE

A Simple Five-Step Approach to
Living Balanced Goals with HEART

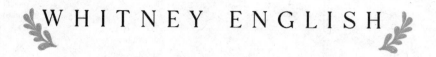

WHITNEY ENGLISH

W PUBLISHING GROUP

AN IMPRINT OF THOMAS NELSON

Published in Nashville, Tennessee, by W Publishing, an imprint of Thomas Nelson.

Thomas Nelson titles may be purchased in bulk for educational, business, fundraising, or sales promotional use. For information, please email SpecialMarkets@ThomasNelson.com.

Scripture quotations are taken from the ESV® Bible (The Holy Bible, English Standard Version®). Copyright © 2001 by Crossway, a publishing ministry of Good News Publishers. Used by permission. All rights reserved.

Any internet addresses, phone numbers, or company or product information printed in this book are offered as a resource and are not intended in any way to be or to imply an endorsement by Thomas Nelson, nor does Thomas Nelson vouch for the existence, content, or services of these sites, phone numbers, companies, or products beyond the life of this book.

ISBN 978-0-7852-5192-7 (HC)
ISBN 978-0-7852-5195-8 (audiobook)
ISBN 978-0-7852-5193-4 (eBook)

Library of Congress Control Number: 2021947723

Printed in the United States of America
22 23 24 25 26 LSC 10 9 8 7 6 5 4 3 2 1

To David, Birch, Truitt, and Charley, the people
who make my life more beautiful.

CONTENTS

INTRODUCTION

"Beauty is a promise of happiness."
ALAIN DE BOTTON[1]

It was Thanksgiving break, 2010—although I use the word *break* here quite loosely. I sat on the edge of the bed at my in-laws' house, looking at my work schedule from that day forward through Christmas. I distinctly remember the deep aubergine walls, my distorted image in the beveled mirror, and the crippling dread in the pit of my stomach. I knew what I was facing. I'd be working extra hours while my family was enjoying turkey dinners and other pre-Christmas festivities. The next month looked like eighteen-hour days and sleeping on the sofa in my office. Something was seriously wrong.

At the time, I owned a stationery business, and holiday cards were our biggest money-maker of the year. This year, we had more orders than ever—which was a good thing, right? As a business owner, you want more orders. But every part of my life was over-leveraged.

My energy.

My time.

My capacity.

My finances (especially my finances).

The stress and uncertainty had thrown my life off-balance. Everything felt like trauma to an already sapped resource. I was discouraged and too tired to do anything about it. I had dreamed of being it all: the perfect wife, mother, daughter, business owner, homekeeper. That's what living the dream meant, right? Doing it all, perfectly, and winning?

But the dream wasn't translating to life. Somebody was missing some memos somewhere. Most of the time, I was stretched, stressed, and steps behind. Life had become a chore. I wondered why on earth I did this to myself.

The most confusing part of all this was: I loved my life—every bit of it! When I wasn't tired, I was grateful for my job, family, home, and projects, even the challenges. I didn't want to quit. I wanted to do it all. But I was missing out on the good life in front of me. Sadly, I wasn't my best self for my family or my job.

A decade has passed since that low point, and during that time I've learned I'm not the only one who has felt the pain of rock bottom. Nearly every woman I talk to has felt something similar. We may not all run businesses, but we all run incredibly complicated, busy lives. We manage our schedules, our kids' schedules, our family's commitments, and our finances. We're the ones coordinating playdates and pick-ups and drop-offs and dinner. For many of us, in addition to working part-time or full-time jobs, we're scheduling doctor's visits, organizing family vacations, and hosting friends for dinner.

We love our families and lives. We're even thankful for the responsibilities! But the reality is, we all have difficult days that somehow stretch into weeks and months, and it all feels like too much.

The day before Thanksgiving, 2010, I felt like the walls of life were closing in on me. I couldn't see a way out. With my fourteen-month-old sleeping in the walk-in closet one wall over, I felt dread, disgust, and discouragement. With a business to run, no energy to do it, and hormones to battle, I began to doubt if I had what it took to live a beautiful life.

How HEART Was Born

I wish I could say I had an epiphany that day in 2010, but even at that low point, I stayed trapped in the turmoil of my own life for a while. However, something inside me was whispering a quiet truth—that life doesn't have to be this frantic. Clinging to this hope helped me reimagine the possibilities of my days, my weeks, and my years. Since then, I've committed to pursue beauty and limit chaos.

Another life is available to you too. It's a joyous life, a meaningful life, deep and full of grace. It isn't tidy, but it shimmers, hollering an invitation and waving a welcoming hand. It won't be as well-curated as the images on social media, but it's full of energy and purpose. It's long-lasting, life-giving, and lovelier than what you've been chasing. It's a life free from the fear of what others will think. It's an abundant heart, overflowing and world rocking.

As I share my story with you, I hope you see yourself and find tangible solutions for quieting your life. Life is beautiful and messy and full of lessons for both of us.

As you read, you'll find stories and strategies about how I turned my life around, using a series of choices that create the acronym HEART: Help yourself, Empower yourself, All your people, Resources and Responsibilities, Trade and Talent. HEART was born out of a deep desire to balance my life. It has evolved into tools, techniques, and tricks that help me plan my day, week, and life. Now, when I see the red flag of chaos I default to HEART. It reminds me to prioritize the present. Because let's face it: life's chaos often obscures what really matters. And when we lose our vision for what could be, our focus on what is, and the motivation to take action, we lose what makes life significant, worthwhile, and beautiful.

HEART represents my attempt to reclaim my life. It's an idea much larger than my imagination. It has gifted me with this not-perfect, always-messy, never-certain life I adore. I want it to be as beneficial to you as it has been to me.

What Is HEART?

We need a new approach to life if we want to live a more beautiful one. After all, the road map we've been following has left some of us in a state of chaos, confusion, and burnout. We can't expect the wrong map to lead us in the right direction: to the deep, fulfilling, peaceful, joyful life we desire. We need a different, simple way to draw our attention away from the noise of everyday life and toward a more balanced and beautiful existence.

My solution was to use the HEART system to prioritize my life. You might call it a method or a framework. Ultimately, it's a way to organize your thoughts that will recharge your imagination, give you hope for the future, and help you stay focused in the present. If you're having a hard time putting your finger on what's wrong with your life—because there's so much that's right—welcome. That's exactly how I felt during that awful Thanksgiving season. As much as I disliked the season, there was still so much to be grateful for.

HEART will help you *design a life you want to live* and help you *live a life designed for you*. It works because it shifts emphasis away from long-term objectives and toward current needs. It works because it's holistic: accounting for both day-to-day life and what's going on in the outside world.

Implementing HEART will help you:

- discover and prioritize what matters most,
- avoid burnout by nourishing your heart,
- make your days meaningful and manageable,
- feel comfortable being who you were created to be,
- develop and grow healthy relationships, and
- dream *better*, not bigger.

I believe HEART is a straightforward strategy you'll enjoy learning and living out every day.

I'm excited to show you how to clarify and organize your dreams and ambitions, with easy and meaningful exercises. Say goodbye to battles of will and scavenging for motivation. Taking action will seem like second nature. You'll feel like your ambitions advance the battle lines for you, as you move forward in reclaiming your beautiful life.

I know this because it worked for me: I still run a business, mother three kids, maintain a marriage, and keep my house (relatively) clean. Even with more obligations and anxieties than ever before, I can wake up with a positive outlook for the day ahead of me (most days). When I'm feeling discouraged, I can get back to the basics. My life is still unruly, but I don't *feel* the chaos in my body and heart the way I used to. Even when things are hectic, I'm okay.

When I look around at my people, my work, and even myself, I see a messy but beautiful thing. It's realistic and authentic, and I wouldn't trade it for the world.

If you're skeptical, I get it. If you had told me about this book back in 2010, I would have rolled my eyes at you (and wondered when a person has time to read books). But if you apply what I show you in this book, I promise you'll get a return on your time. Promise.

You'll uncover ideas for routines, hacks for habits, clarity on what to cut and what to keep. You'll discover a cadence in your life, a consistency, a rhythm to your days and weeks and months, a discipline that doesn't feel like drudgery or punishment, and a structure that will delight your inner child. HEART will give you permission to quiet self-judgment, grow your belief in yourself, and open your eyes to the idea that we've been hurting ourselves by running after things that won't satisfy our souls.

Goal-Setting vs. Goal-Living

Although the idea for HEART was born out of my desire to set better goals (more on that later), this book is more about goal-living rather than goal-setting.

Goal-setting is about getting or achieving something you don't already have. It's a destination—a new house, a better car, a promotion, a marathon finished—as if more is the answer. I came to this realization slowly: for those who already have so much (maybe even too much), more is rarely the answer.

Goal-living is different. Goal-living is about peace of mind and personal internal reward. Goal-living is about seeing your life with a fresh perspective. It offers grace, and with it the confidence that you've done your best and are living out your purpose. Goal-living comes with the knowledge that you're helping others while enjoying your journey. You won't feel imbalanced or off-center as you pursue one arena of your life, left with a nagging feeling you've forgotten something and will pay for it later.

I don't want to mislead you. I'm not saying goals are bad, but I do want to shake up the subculture surrounding them. There's a whole host of lingo: "breaking down goals," "setting" them, "tracking" them—this is the stuff I'm telling you to step away from. The language of productivity and focus is not a prerequisite for living a beautiful and fulfilled life. And for many of us, it's become a distraction.

Say you've always wanted to lose fifteen pounds, and in your mind you'll be miserable until you do—and if you don't, then that's just it. But what if, instead, you focused on what makes you feel good today? Instead of your desired final weight, what if you focused on the next best choice? Maybe eating a healthy meal or moving your body? Before you realize it, you're living out your goal, rather than waiting in agony for the end result to materialize.

It's not about the absence of goals, or the presence of goals. Our focus should be on our *lives*, not our goals. When we look at it that way, we don't need goals as much as we thought we did.

Achieving our goals is not a onetime choice and a big jump forward. It's loads of little decisions that add up over time. The good news is, when we step into understanding our needs, we'll have the proper mindset in place to make it easy to keep going.

Goal-living isn't the path of more. It's the path of better.

Our Roadmap

In Part I, we'll meet HEART and I'll share more about how it came to be. We will discover the skills necessary to reveal our current thought processes, empowering us to design a strategy that works with our personalities and aligns with our priorities and intentions. We'll get things out of our heads and onto paper so we have clear minds and a clean slate for Part II.

In Part II, we will review each letter of HEART, the Life Segments. The questions in the prompts at the end of each chapter will pinpoint our needs and inspire our goal ideas. Work through these as you go. You'll have five lists, and you may want to compile them before moving to Part III.

Part III is practical and chock-full of ideas for our systems, schedules, and lives. Using our five lists from Part II, we'll transfer our needs and goal ideas onto the Goal Grid. The Goal Grid is a handy one-page tool for keeping our schedules organized and on track. We'll use HEART to look at both long-term goals and a daily to-do list. HEART can simplify our weeks, months, or decades. I've also compiled my favorite organizing hacks to help you in your most overwhelmed moments.

I want this to be easy and enjoyable for you. My desire is to get you on the right track, because so many of us are off track due to how we've been setting our goals. You don't need anything except this book and your favorite pen to get started. Along the way, if you feel prompted to write more, grab a journal. If you want to take it a step further, pull out your planner when you get to Part III.

At the end of each chapter is a section called "Write It Down, Make It Beautiful." The questions and exercises vary by chapter. I encourage you to pull out a journal and use these as writing prompts. Journaling has been a big part of implementing HEART into my life, and I think it will work for you as well. These questions will lead you through reflection, brainstorming, and planning.

You might be tempted to jump straight ahead to the implementation chapters. But hold on there, speed racer. You are smart enough to resist the quick-fix sales pitch of perfectly productive lives. If you want lasting results, you know this will take some heart work, some soul-searching, and (dare I say) some navel-gazing. We are talking about finding the good life in the here and now, not in some far-off destination you think will make you happy. We will unpack what you need to embrace this present moment.

I want you to meet yourself on these pages. I encourage you to write in the book, in the margins, or on the endpapers. "When we write, a unique neural circuit is automatically activated," says psychologist Stanislas Dehaene. "There is a core recognition of the gesture in the written word, a sort of recognition by mental simulation in your brain."[2]

There is no right answer to the questions I'll offer. I'm simply asking them to get you thinking and help you shift your perspective. Within these pages, you'll find answers within yourself you didn't know you had. You'll discover solutions to and acceptance of the things that have been plaguing you. Your path out of chaos and into a beautiful life will be unique. Make this book yours.

The Path to a Beautiful Life

You purchased this book because you're looking for a strategy that works. Maybe you tried goal-setting and failed, and you don't want to try again. Or maybe this is your first time attempting the goals.

If this book does anything for you, I want it to give you encouragement and inspiration to chase a life designed by you, for you—your one and only exquisite, priceless, all-too-short life. I want it to help you see the magnificence in the world, and in your community, but also your potential—which, by the way, I believe is almost infinite. And I want it to give you hope, because that is what we need far more than a fully executed to-do list.

Self-help books on how to identify your priorities, set goals, break them down, create an action plan, and schedule everything are plentiful. The problem is, I've yet to find a book that tells me how to do this in a way that fits with an actual Tuesday.

And yes, life is hard no matter how well we organize it. But in my view, there are two kinds of hard—necessary hard and unnecessary hard. This book will alleviate (some of) the unnecessary hard. In that way, I do believe it will make the process seem easy. It will become a rich resource for finding motivation and perspective when our journey gets dark.

I wrote this for busy, tired women struggling to design a life they love. This book is for anyone who has ever struggled to balance profession and play, people and projects, pets and provisions. Productivity advice is overflowing, but I wanted to pave a clear path for those who want to manage everyday duties while staying connected to the HEART of what they do. Whether you are employed or an entrepreneur, fur-ball mom or kid mom, or a combination of all the above, I know you've (at times) felt frustrated and trapped inside the chaos of a life that you know could be beautiful. Me too.

With the help of this book, you can learn to run a business, a dishwasher, and a marathon simultaneously (but only if you want to). More importantly, HEART can show you how to love yourself, your people, and your circumstances.

Whatever you choose to do, you'll be doing it with HEART.

We need to see our lives through the lens of possibility. We deserve a life that doesn't burn us out in a month or work just long enough to make us look good on Instagram. HEART will direct us to that life: not a perfect one, but a balanced one that will lead us to rich, meaningful abundance.

This is your path to a more beautiful life.

PART I

Chapter 1

GOALS GONE WRONG

"My goal is no longer to get more done, but rather to have less to do."
FRANCINE JAY[1]

I remember where I was sitting when the mail came on July 17, 2012. The scrappy office building where my company set up camp was formerly a flooring showroom. The carpet changed every twenty feet, with wood or tile options interjecting. When the mailman came, he hopped inside over a circle of tile, dropped the mail, and waved. From a heavily decorated kidney-shaped desk (thanks to the scratch and dent at the local furniture mecca), I waved back.

Without a budget for new flooring, we made do. I stepped onto the orange oak, crossing a confused matrix of brown walnut and yellow pineslabs. Mahogany bookcases behind me clashed in contrast, waiting for our financial situation to improve.

For almost two years, maybe three, I'd been living paycheck to paycheck—except that's not really accurate because I hadn't been paying myself. Whatever was in the business checking account went to employees, vendors, bills, and credit cards. There simply wasn't anything left over for me. As a business owner, wife, and mom, it was a nightmare.

Rifling through the stack of mail, I remembered when the business used to have energy and excitement and cash flow. All that was gone now. Dreams of old victories had kept me going, hoping for better days. I was afraid to face reality or acknowledge the operation was failing, the wheels attached to the car with paper clips and string.

After the friendly carrier dropped the mail that day, I got up from my desk to riffle through it. Every invoice-I-could-barely-pay and past due notice reminded me that I was failing. And then I came across a thicker, linen-textured envelope. It was distinctive—heavier, foreboding. I did not want to open it.

My admission that the company was in a vulnerable position had come only weeks earlier. Daily, my straggling team and I managed to hold the rattletrap together, but I knew if we were to unexpectedly get a flat or the transmission were to go out or the muffler fell off, the charade would be over. Maybe you've found yourself in a position like this—not with a business but with a marriage or finances or a challenging relationship. Where it feels like you're barely hanging on. If you can relate, you'll know what I mean when I say: we could handle any setback, but only one setback at a time. More than two disasters at once had the potential to take down my already-weak operation.

I held the ecru envelope with an attorney's address printed in tan ink on the top left-hand corner and drew out the trifold paper. Unfolded, I recognized the gist of it in an instant.

Years prior, one of our largest customers had allowed their invoices to accumulate well past due dates, and in the ninety days prior to filing bankruptcy, they had tried to settle their account with my business. It was for less than the amount they owed, but still significant, so we took it and counted our blessings.

This notice came bearing bad news about that big check. Since the company had filed bankruptcy less than ninety days after sending the settlement check, the trustee of their bankruptcy legally had the right to come to us and ask for that money back—even though it had been years since the transaction. It's what they call a "bankruptcy rollback."

Here was the problem: we didn't have the money. I sat, staring at the reality in front of me—the trustee was demanding we pay this large sum of money back, money we simply didn't have. I knew what this meant. I didn't want to believe it yet, but I knew.

I was usually fairly resourceful about coming up with answers, finding alternatives, and maneuvering my way to desired results. But this time, this problem, well, I don't think even MacGyver had enough paper clips to keep the car together.

We had only one choice: file bankruptcy on the business and close. I would have to call our creditors—many of whom I considered friends—and admit we were broke. I offered pennies on the dollar before finally closing the doors. The whole thing felt dirty and plain wrong.

You likely haven't filed for bankruptcy before. Although it is devastating for those who have, it's not a universal problem. But the devastation I felt is universal. Deep shame. Crippling fear. And the general sense that somewhere, somehow, I had made a massive, uncorrectable mistake.

Something had to change. Not just closing the business—something else. But I couldn't put my finger on it. Life wasn't going as planned, and I couldn't figure out why.

It wasn't the bankruptcy that leveled me as much as it was what the bankruptcy revealed for me. I was beyond burnt-out, way past stressed, and my life wasn't one I was proud of or could enjoy. I was disappointed with myself and frustrated with my circumstances, so far from what I pictured for my life. Despite having the beautiful family I had always dreamed of, a home that was messy but comfortable, and pursuing the career of my (I thought) dreams, I was miles and miles away from any sense of peace.

Every day was fraught with fear and plagued with panic, as I rushed about, trying to do it all, and doing none of it well. It was chaos.

And the business was only part of it. I was behind on bathroom cleaning, burning dinners, and battling depression. I didn't feel in control—and I didn't feel like me.

Maybe this was just motherhood? Being an entrepreneur? Maybe everyone else felt this overwhelmed and out of control but wasn't saying anything? Or maybe *I* was the problem.

Sitting at my desk, weary, discouraged, and facing a string of problems I didn't know how to manage, the one thing I knew for sure was that I wanted a different life. It didn't even matter what kind of life—as long as it wasn't this one.

I wanted to feel empowered to accomplish everything on my plate. I wanted to know everything was going to be okay. I wanted to feel present instead of distracted, successful instead of like a deadbeat, caught up instead of behind. I wanted time at the end of the day to enjoy my family and friends. I aspired to be the person I had promised my family I could be.

What was I doing wrong? How had I arrived here? How could I be failing so epically?

Failure is painful, but long ago I decided that if I could find a lesson in a harrowing experience, then it would at least count for education. I sat at my desk, staring at that fancy envelope, dreading the next few weeks of embarrassing phone calls, and mentally resolving not to waste this failure. I call it an MBA from the School of Hard Knocks. Experience is the best teacher, and I decided to believe—as absurd as it sounds—that this was my chance to take a step back and analyze what went wrong and why.

I might have failed at everything else. But that much I got right.

As I reflected, I pulled out my goal notebook—a binder I've kept since college—and reviewed my past goals. I've always been career-oriented, as evidenced by several of my ambitions: the desire to hit a specific dollar amount in sales, be featured in the national press, build a website, and grow the blog. I had some personal goals recorded too: run a 5k, lose ten pounds, read more books. Pulling out my planner, I saw a list of memories I wanted to make: family Easter, the neighborhood Halloween shindig, our murder mystery New Year's Eve party, and a family road trip.

These were all good things, things I believed I could do. So how did the list of dreams before me—things that made me feel excited and energized and creative and in love—add up to a life I loathed?

What's Possible?

The world is short on fairy godmothers and pixie dust, and I've been to enough estate sales to say with confidence that brass oil lamps don't come with genies. Or magic. It's up to us to make it happen in this life. We all recognized this at one point or another in our lives, and when we asked someone to tell us how to do it, they told us to set goals.

As if goal-setting is the answer.

Somewhere along the line, I picked up the belief that if I achieve as much as possible, I'll be happy. As women, we daily take on this challenge with impossible expectations of ourselves—and because we're incredible, we crush them.

We dash from responsibility to responsibility, hoping to reach the finish line before we collapse. Frankly, we're good at managing it all. Watch any of us in action: people, projects, deadlines, and dishwashing fill our days. We plan meetings, drive car pool, juggle clients, sign up for Pilates classes, and check email. We schedule doctor, dentist, and hairdresser appointments. We compose grocery lists that sound like sonnets.

We are capable of doing it all. But in the frenzy, we forget to ask ourselves: *How are we doing?* Like, *really* doing?

The answer to this question is where we've gone wrong.

We've said we're fine, and we're not.

In setting our goals, we've also set ourselves up for failure.

To be fair, I'm not saying we shouldn't have ambitions. I'm a woman with big dreams and I don't plan on letting those go anytime soon. But if we're setting our goals without HEART, then even if we achieve them, we might lose ourselves in the process. Achievements make for a great first impression, but when we prioritize them ahead of our needs, we run the risk of waking up in the middle of the night, plagued by the question: *Do I even like my life?*

No matter how many productivity apps we try, we still end the day worn out. Time-management strategies provide short-term relief, but then a sick day throws a wrench in our plans and a crowbar on our dreams. We stay on track with our goals for a month, and then we're derailed by life's infamous hiccups: a sick kid, a fender bender, or getting snapped at by someone else who also has a full plate.

With a typical goal-setting method, these curveballs threaten to steal our joy and permeate our souls with remorse and regret. Because, again, we're focused on the goal. What I want to share—and what I've learned since that fateful day in 2012—is that these curveballs don't have to change the way we feel about ourselves.

Because it's not about the goal, it's about the HEART.

The solution to our exhaustion may not be as simple as taking things off our already overflowing plates. Aside from reducing the volume of tasks, let's examine and ask ourselves whether the way we organize and prioritize our days is beneficial or detrimental. Often it's not the elements of our lives making us unhappy, but our approach to them.

Our goals are not the problem. The way we try to achieve those goals needs to change.

SMART Goals and Why They Fail Us

When I was in high school, the state of Oklahoma hosted a workshop retreat for seniors. The top seniors from schools across Oklahoma gathered at a camp for a two-night retreat to talk leadership, goals, ambitions, and the like. Students were selected based on athletic involvement and grade point average.

Translation: *not me.*

But it just so happened that the retreat weekend coincided with a series of other events so that *every other student in my class* could not attend the retreat. The smart kids had an event, the athletes had a tournament—which meant the school was left with the challenge of selecting a student who was neither smart nor athletic.

Enter Whitney, stage left.

There's nothing like getting to hang out with smart and athletic people when you are neither smart nor athletic. But in short, the weekend was fantastic. Turns out, smart and athletic kids liked me anyway! Maybe I'm funny, who knows. New friends exchanged addresses to write letters (because it was the 1900s, as my kids say). I drank all the leadership, goal, and ambition Kool-Aid served. I've been a retreat, conference, and workshop junkie ever since.

I soon learned the universal fact that all conferences, workshops, and retreats have a goal-setting talk, session, or speaker. During this segment, the speaker says, "Imagine what your life will look like in ten years." You look at your paper, or notebook, swag pen poised to write, and go straight for the big guns: family, spouse, dream house, dream car, solid bank account, great body, world travels, contentment, and happiness. Big dreams.

The speaker then asks you to write five-year goals. "A few," he says, and you question the ambiguity of the task. Looking at your big dreams, you chop them in half: save money for the dream house/car, work some overtime for savings, join a gym?

The speaker asks you to repeat the task.

"What's your one-year goal?" Ideas are roughly chopped in half again, and at this point you are wondering when the plan and to-do list will magically appear.

If you've ever done anything like this (at a conference or at home sitting on your bed), welcome to the club. We're following this template for a reason.

Whether knowingly or not, we can trace our approach to personal achievement back to a prominent method that has defined the goal-setting space since the eighties. This system asks for discipline and promises results. It's extremely popular, and its memorable acronym has made its way into everyday vernacular.

It's SMART goals. The methodology created by George Duran debuted in the November 1981 issue of *Management Review*, a business journal. In the two-page article, he explained that in corporate culture, there is a "SMART" way to write goals and objectives, with details of what each letter stands for:

Specific: target a specific area for improvement.
Measurable: quantify or suggest an indicator of progress.
Assignable: specify who will do it. (Later interpretations changed this to "Achievable.")
Realistic: state what results can realistically be achieved, given available resources.
Time-related: specify when the result(s) can be achieved.

Even if you're not explicitly using SMART goals, chances are, your approach to life goals have been influenced in some way by this acronym. It's popular and it seems straightforward. Pick a place you want to go, divide it up into parts, and see where you need to be at each increment of time.

We've been told that goal-setting is the only way to achieve what we want, so we've applied SMART liberally. We've turned it into an acquisition strategy. This method must be the key to the next promotion, bigger house, better relationships, and healthier physique. I want to run a marathon next June, so I break down the goal. I want to make a million dollars next year, so I project quarterly. I'd like to be married by thirty-five, so I turn it into a numbers game.

These achievement techniques may work in the sense that they do tend to get us to an identified goal. But what we miss in this kind of goal-setting is how we feel about our lives in the process. How much does reaching the objective matter if we don't feel good about our lives along the way (or even at the finish line)?

What if there's something missing that could make all this function and feel better?

Before my business took a downhill turn, I made a choice I now believe cost me greatly. I googled "SMART goals" and made a list in the hopes that it would get me out of the pickle I was in.

As my life became busier and felt more out of control, instead of stopping and checking in on myself, I did what I had been taught to do: I doubled down on my goal-setting efforts. I looked at where I wanted to be, I set goals, I broke down those goals into smaller pieces, and I finished the tasks I'd been told would make these dreams come to pass.

And this set me up for disaster.

The SMART goals theory touts itself as a tried-and-true life strategy, but one of the most frequently cited studies about goal-setting in general is an urban myth. It goes something like this: "Less than 3 percent of Yale's graduating class of 1953 documented their post-graduation goals. Thirty years later, that 3 percent had a higher net worth than the other 97 percent." Except it's not true; no such study ever existed. Yale's own library web page dispels the myth.[2]

Even if it were true, I'd want to know about the quality of life of that 3 percent as much as I'd want to know about their net worth. Do they have a loving spouse? Feel connected to their kids? Enjoy their profession? Feel supported by their extended family? This goes without saying, but there's more to life than net worth.

Even if you want to die on the hill of traditional goal-setting, the fact remains, even the most committed among us don't always act on our goals in a way that helps us achieve them. A University of Scranton study found only 8 percent of people who set goals took enough action on their goals to achieve them. The other 92 percent failed.[3]

A MORE BEAUTIFUL LIFE

There were several reasons why participants failed:

- The participant procrastinated on taking steps to make progress.
- The goal implementation plan was inflexible and did not allow for adjustment.
- The participant did not have the physical or emotional capacity for the goal.
- The participant became bored with their goal.
- The participant's goal was based on other people's expectations.
- The participant made no plan as to how to achieve the goal.
- The participant did not create any accountability for themselves.

Does any of this sound familiar to you? It does to me. Procrastination, lack of accountability, lack of capacity, lack of personal connection to the goal, life getting in the way—this pretty much describes my 2012 demise. So why did I keep turning to this method that was clearly not working?

Goal-setting is a win-lose, zero-sum game of me versus my goals. If I fail, the goal wins. If I succeed, I win. No in-between, and points for effort are not allowed. Not to mention, I can't control the curveballs, further increasing the odds of goal failure. I'm tired of failing at my goals!

But consider this: What if it's not our goals that are failing us, but the way we're managing our goals? What if we approached goals (and life) differently, focusing less on the outcome and more on the process? Could there be a more flexible method to priorities and progress?

Maybe there can be.

On some level, I get it: the SMART goals acronym is catchy. In fact, it's so catchy that it comes in almost endless iterations. Some goal gurus have gone so far as to add letters: you can now set SMARTER goals! It's memorable.

I will even admit that SMART goals can be useful in some situations. Think about this for a second: Duran wrote SMART goals for a business publication, to help managers better monitor and improve employee performance. SMART goals are meant for business and career— and in my humble opinion, that's where they belong. It's not that SMART goals won't get us anywhere; it's that they don't guarantee us a more beautiful, meaningful, fulfilling life. They're "head goals," not HEART goals filled with hope and truth and joy.

Call it goal-setting, goal-living, prioritizing, or productivity. HEART is a new and refreshing way to frame our tasks, to-dos, and troubles, because let's be real: SMART goals aren't cutting it. We've been sabotaging ourselves since 1982, you guys. We are in desperate need of an upgrade.

It might be helpful to know before we dive in that I'm a Christian. My faith influences how I process my circumstances and what I believe makes life meaningful. If you're also a Christian, you'll be more familiar with the examples I use, the way I talk about God, and how I've ordered my priorities. If you're not a Christian, know that I've done my best to make this book just as welcoming and relevant to you, while staying true to my convictions. Please feel free to replace my words or examples with ones that make sense to you in your faith perspective.

Faith and spirituality may be a sensitive subject for some. I'm not here to debate the existence of God; I'm simply here to declare that my life is less chaotic when I accept that I'm not in charge. This material is intended to help you identify and eliminate any obstacle to living beautifully. The wonderful part about pursuing Truth is that Truth isn't afraid of your questions. If you pursue it, you'll find it.

A Vision, Not a Goal

If you're like me, right now you are questioning a book that steers you away from goals. After all, you're an ambitious person who *wants* to do it all (zero shame). You just don't want to feel like an empty shell at the end of the day because your goal drained your soul. I promise I won't ask you to give up your dreams—or your idealism—about all you can accomplish in life or how amazing you hope it will be. I want to help you achieve those goals without selling your soul.

If you're willing to go on this journey with me, I'll show you how you can achieve everything you wanted to achieve (and probably more) while staying grounded, connected, and energized from the inside out.

It's not about thinking small. Quite the opposite. It's about thinking bigger than ever before. We do this by using visions rather than goals.

Andy Stanley describes vision as something "born in the soul of a man or woman who is consumed with the tension between what is and what could be."[4] Visions don't come to those distracted by daydreams, nor do they come to those racing through reality. It takes a willingness to slow down and reflect—recognizing *what is* and *what could be*—to have a vision. (Which, by the way, is exactly what we'll learn how to do in this book.)

To further explain what he means by vision, Stanley tells the story of Nehemiah from the Scriptures.[5]

Nehemiah was a Jew living abroad, serving as a high servant to the king. The city of Jerusalem was in ruins, and the people had drifted away from their beliefs, customs, and laws. Nehemiah didn't justify the situation, or ignore it by busying himself with tasks. Instead, he recognized it for what it was: the relaxed practices had weakened the people, and the physical ruin had left the city vulnerable and exposed.

Nehemiah asked how the city and people were faring (i.e., he sought to know what was).

Moreover, Nehemiah anticipated *what should have been*: those walls and gates should have been strong, solid, and high—a physical form of protection, as well as a symbol of strength and unity. The people should have followed their laws and customs, prospering instead of suffering. This dichotomy between what was and what should have been gave him a vision for restoring Jerusalem to its previous glory.

Let's apply this to our lives, looking first at *what is*. Be honest with yourself about where you are, and don't be afraid to dig deep.

What are your highlights and achievements, your moments of pride, joy, or contentment? Where do you struggle or fall short? How are you hurting? Lastly, what is the middle ground, your day-to-day grind? We're all complex, and life isn't all extremes. No one's list should be all good or all bad. If your list skews one way or another, bring in people you trust to help you round out the picture.

Now, let's talk about *what could be.*

Looking at your *what is* list, is anything heartbreaking, embarrassing, or causing a guilt trip? Do you ever feel like you've settled for far less than you're capable of or deserve? What could this list look like instead? (Note that Andy Stanley didn't say *what would be agreeable,* or *what we think would be best for us,* or *what isn't possible even in a perfect world.* He said *what could be.*)

Once you've examined *what is* and determined *what could be,* you can begin building your visions on that dichotomy.

Nehemiah's vision was for a restored Jerusalem, both its walls and its people. Given the state it was in, that must have seemed remarkable. Yet, he shared his vision by asking the king to allow him to return to Jerusalem and restore it. He fought fiercely against all the forces that wished to fail him. And he succeeded. The wall was rebuilt in only fifty-two days, and the people were restored to their former practices, success, and unity.

Nehemiah was successful because he saw what was, sought what could have been, and acted on the vision in his heart.

What are your hopes and dreams for your life now that you've thought about what is and what could be?

When you feel connected to a greater purpose and other people, when you have a sense of gratitude and meaning, and when you have the strength to handle stress and unforeseen circumstances, you will have the energy and stamina to build a beautiful life.

What We Lose When We Set Goals the Old Way

From my point of view, the biggest mistake we make when we set goals is that we sacrifice a beautiful present for the sake of an arbitrary future.

Let me explain what I mean.

Onstage, the speaker asks you to write down your goals. "What do you want?" they prompt. Then, "Where do you want to end up in life?" So, you reflect, and write what comes to mind (the goal weight, the goal house, the perfect party, the promotion).

However, no matter how thoughtfully or intentionally we approach this task, the process still leads us to set what I refer to as *arbitrary goals*. Influenced by the culture around us, the goals we scribble in those few minutes likely are not things that would bring us true, rich, and deep fulfillment. They're things that you think you should have, things that you've been told will make you happy, things other people have, or things other people want you to have.

Arbitrary goals can also be called comparison goals: goals based on what other people are pursuing or what other people tell us we should do. These goals have little to no connection to the life we are actually living. They have little to no connection to who we *are*. They do not consider the very real limitations of our lives (how much free time we have, how many kids we have, what our home responsibilities are, if we're taking care of our aging parents).

Our goals set us up for failure if we create them without first considering if they would enhance our lives or make us happy as we work toward them. Traditional goal-setting positions us for failure because it begins with the head and belittles the heart.

Furthermore, setting the goal (naming it) is often where we stop. We spend our energy on naming what we want (or what we think we're supposed to want) without spending any energy on how we will get there.

Allow me to use an example from *South Park*: one character makes a business plan, illustrated on a board in three phases. Phase 1 is to collect underpants. Phase 3 is to turn a profit. But as the character is questioned about the plan, the viewer realizes that there is no phase 2. They have no idea how to turn their collection of underpants into a profitable business—and yet, they have started phase 1 with enthusiasm (as evidenced by the characters eagerly throwing underpants into a pile).[6]

Not many of us are trying to turn a profit from underpants (and maybe even fewer enjoy *South Park*), so let's try another example.

Suzy decides she's going to lose eighteen pounds. This doesn't seem like an arbitrary goal, at first glance. She has calculated inches, pounds, calories, macros, workouts, and weeks, and her doctor told her this was essential. She plans, dividing the goal into weeks, pounds, and days, and posts the number eighteen around the house in circumspect alcoves to remind herself. After seven days, the scale doesn't show a decrease—the darn thing must be broken, because it can't be possible that it would go the other way! Suzy looks at her calculations and frowns. She is not on track to achieve her goal. In fact, she is going the opposite direction.

To ward off the emotions of failure, Suzy decides this whole goal thing, weight loss thing, and general self-improvement thing is a marketing hoax. She knows that next week she'll feel so bad about herself, she might as well order the donuts now.

What went wrong for *South Park* and Suzy isn't that they lacked vision: both parties knew what they wanted (profit up, pounds down). It wasn't that they lacked focus, even if *South Park* was missing a step. It was that neither of them addressed the process—the messy middle part with all the obstacles.

- How would the process look and feel to them?
- How would this fit in their actual (not hypothetical) life?
- How would they cope when life got in the way and progress didn't happen as planned?
- How did they want to *feel*—regardless of the outcome?

We've set ourselves up for failure by committing to arbitrary goals, by ignoring crucial aspects of our lives, and by not considering how the achievement method fits into our everyday lives. We blame ourselves for lack of effort or discipline, beating ourselves up and compounding our anxiety. This is not an "us" problem. Failure to reach our goals is often not a failure of our efforts or discipline. The root of the issue resides in the relationship between brain function and goal-system.

When we believe that the "good life" will only come after we have achieved some certain goal (especially an arbitrary one), our brains tell us we're unsafe. What happens is that our amygdala (aka the lizard brain)—the part of our brain responsible for fear—perceives that we won't be safe until we achieve the goal. Until we accomplish the goal, the amygdala will keep sending us warnings.[7] You've probably gotten some of these.

It whispers, *You have not arrived yet; it's not time to rest yet.* No wonder we're tired! Our brains won't let us rest until we've achieved our goals. Worse yet, we keep trying to solve this problem by setting more goals!

You might say to yourself, *Well, I've achieved several of the goals I set—and I never could have done that without the SMART goals method.* Of course, that's partly true (for me too). But have you ever noticed how, when we achieve success, the bar goes up? It's not like you achieve something great (running a half-marathon, for instance) and then suddenly feel better about yourself. No. You feel better about yourself for a moment, but it fades, especially when the flyer for the full marathon shows up.

You recalibrate, walk through another goal-setting session, track the goals, and raise the bar. Again.

Perhaps you've felt like me, finding it difficult to find joy and contentment and a meaning-ful life in that process. And why should we have to wait until we achieve or accumulate or arrive to be happy? Why can't we enjoy our lives *right now*?

The good stuff of life, the stuff the good Lord intended for us (fulfillment, love, joy, mean-ing, happiness, growth, beauty) are not locations at which we can arrive. Wonder, adventure, and abundance are part of the process, not prizes we win when we've checked the boxes. These rich delights were not intended to be pursued as payoffs.

We are designed to *live* a beautiful life. Not spend all of our time and energy chasing after it.

When used for personal goal-setting, SMART goals can be a recipe for disaster. You may feel like living proof of that right now. But this is where HEART has a secret sauce: it's not built upon destination or arbitrary wants. It doesn't hinge on a specific outcome. Instead of asking what I want or where I want to go, it asks a simple, alternative question, empowering me to chart a course and embrace the process: *What do I need?*

Take a minute to respond to the questions below. Reflect on your earlier experiences with goal-setting, what has worked for you, and how you feel about your life now.

1. How do you feel about your life right now? Consider *what is* and *what could be.*
2. Have you achieved any big goals in the past? What has worked and what hasn't?
3. Do you have a current goal list? If so, what does it look like?

Chapter 2

HEART EXPLAINED

"And so, rock bottom became the solid
foundation on which I rebuilt my life."
J.K. ROWLING[1]

A beautiful life doesn't come from accomplishments: from a perfectly clean house, finishing a marathon, a career promotion, or even from the dream vacation with your family. Ordinary, everyday moments are the building blocks of a beautiful life. Each and every moment, no matter how mundane or unexceptional, serves as the foundation for an extraordinary life. When we are fully present we can appreciate and find joy in those moments. Only then will we discover a truly beautiful life.

It's not that accomplishments can't be meaningful.

The problem is when we let an arbitrary goal become more important than the life that's in front of us. The one we're living now. Perhaps you can relate.

- We stay up late, then get up early until we're exhausted—without ever evaluating why we want to achieve the goal in the first place.
- We sacrifice ourselves and time with the people we love for the sake of the project.
- We're so focused on the accomplishment that we let the little tasks pile up.

Eventually, those little tasks become the chaos in our days (no clean clothes, the car runs out of gas, the house must be cleaned for company thirty minutes before they arrive, there's no food in the fridge).

If working toward these accomplishment-driven SMART goals is causing you to feel anxious, out of control, and continually frustrated with your present life, then these goals aren't making your life better—even if they're helping you achieve the end objective.

To reiterate, I'm not asking you to give up your dreams. Your mission, should you choose to accept it, is to try this HEART thing on for size. See if it makes your life less chaotic and more balanced, leaving space for goodness and love and joy and simple pleasures.

As cliché as it sounds, it's true: a beautiful life is a result of finding fulfillment in the journey. That means less chaos, more peace, more of what fills you up, and more of what makes a difference in your days. Rather than focusing on what we want to achieve, we should look at what we need to discover these essential components for a rich and fulfilling life.

Human Needs: What Runs Our Lives

What do I mean by "needs"? Very simply, needs are whatever keeps you going and whatever makes your life run. Needs are the activities that keep you, a human, surviving and thriving. What's crazy is how many of us (myself included) are *ignoring* our needs in favor of our wants (the marathon, the promotion, the vacation). This is backward, of course, and I wonder why it didn't dawn on me sooner.

When we neglect our needs, life slowly slips into more chaos.

Yet, in our frenetic pace, we frequently push our needs aside or don't even allow them to register. Consider this: how many times have you skipped a meal, gone an entire day without drinking enough water, slept less than eight hours per night, or told yourself to suck it up and be an adult when all you needed was a good cry?

When was the last time you talked to a therapist or counselor, read a self-help book, or humbled yourself to ask for help from a mentor or wise friend? When did you last spend time meditating, praying, or reading to renew your spirit and transform your mind?

What about setting a necessary boundary with a demanding coworker or friend? How often have your kids asked to spend time with you lately? How many times have you said yes? When was the last time you went on a date with your significant other? How long has it been since you met up with a "pick up where you left off" friend and had a meaningful, rich, soul-filling conversation?

Do you ever procrastinate on tasks that help you manage your life and care for yourself and your family? The chores, the bills, the honey-do list, the tidying?

When was the last time you evaluated your work or your passion projects? Have you neglected something that brings you energy and joy? Is your career overtaking your life?

Health, emotional stability, relationships, life responsibilities, and work: these are all examples of what keep us, as humans, going.

I didn't make this up. If you think back to your Psychology 101 class, you'll likely remember a guy named Abraham Maslow and his pyramid: the Hierarchy of Needs. Each of the pyramid's levels represents a set of human needs. The central idea is that some needs are more fundamental than others. He grouped these essentials into five categories:

Level 1: Physiological needs: food, rest, clothing, water, air
Level 2: Safety and security: resources, health, shelter
Level 3: Belonging: love and acceptance
Level 4: Esteem: prestige and accomplishment
Level 5: Self-actualization: creative fulfillment[2]

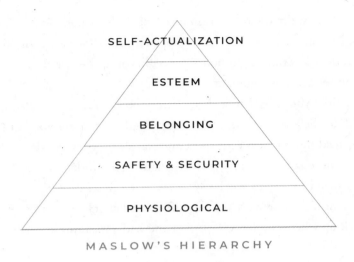

MASLOW'S HIERARCHY

Maslow proposed that you can't advance to the next level until you've met your needs at the previous one. That is, if my basic sense of safety and survival is jeopardized, I cannot seek more advanced needs like love and acceptance. And if I don't feel loved and accepted, I can't achieve creative fulfillment or reach my potential.

And yet, we regularly attempt to bypass Maslow's first three levels to attain levels four and five. The effect it has had on us is obvious. The hierarchy of needs provides a common foundation for all people, regardless of circumstances, successes, or failures. We have needs, and disregarding them will have a negative impact on our well-being.

Addressing needs rather than desires will lead to a happier and more fulfilling existence. This may come as a surprise to those who have been told you can "be anything you want to be" and all you have to do is "put your mind to something and you can achieve it." This is sound advice, but it won't help if you don't first attend to your needs. There is a deficit until needs are met: one step forward, two steps back.

So, how do we break free from our natural tendency to pursue our desires without first satisfying our needs? Enter: HEART.

HEART

This is where HEART can help us. Born out of the need for a flexible, forgiving system, and developed through a chaotic season, HEART has been fine-tuned and adapted over the years.

I prefer to think of HEART as a checklist of essentials rather than a goal-setting system. Even more, it has evolved into a life management system for weekly and monthly planning, as well as daily self–check-ins.

HEART quickly reminds us of our basic needs when we're feeling off-track. HEART maximizes our time, energy, talents, and resources, empowering us to achieve the things we *want*, *after* our needs have been met. The journey may surprise you, though. Have you ever gotten what you wanted, only to realize it wasn't what you wanted at all? Start with what you need, not what you want, to get what your heart truly desires.

In simplest terms, HEART is a life management system. The structure adheres to Maslow's hierarchy of needs, but that was an accidental discovery on my part. Each letter in the HEART acronym represents an area of your life—the Life Segments.

HEART asks:

- What do I need to manage my physical well-being?
- What do I need to meet my emotional, mental, and spiritual well-being?
- What do I need to do to enrich my relationships?
- What do I need to steward my resources and responsibilities well?
- What do I need to do with my gifts and abilities to serve my community best?

It's important to note the order: basic, primitive, and daily physical needs are first—needs we often ignore! Imagine the strong foundation you could build if you recognized these requirements, satisfied them first, and then moved your way to the next level.

Life Segment 1: Help Yourself: Physiological and safety needs; including food, rest, health, and well-being

Life Segment 2: Empower Yourself: Emotional, mental, and spiritual needs; some hobbies, education, personal development, mindset

Life Segment 3: All Your People: Social needs; needs related to your family, spouse, and community; belonging, love, and acceptance

Life Segment 4: Resources and Responsibilities: Household chores, transportation logistics and responsibilities, and financial tasks

Life Segment 5: Trade and Talent: Prestige and accomplishment, career, ambitions; the stuff of traditional goal-setting

It's hard to see in the pyramid (since it's upside down) but the acronym looks like this:

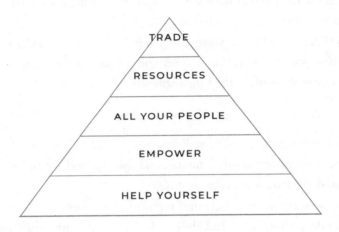

HEART MODEL

H—Help Yourself

Four checkpoints foster a strong base in *Help Yourself.* Each component is essential for our physical well-being: sleep, nutrition, water, and movement.

Think about what you can accomplish when your body is well-nourished with the essentials for life. Can you visualize yourself well-rested, nourished, hydrated, and fit? How does your current reality differ from that visual? Sleep gets pushed to the wayside for "when things slow down"; you somehow make it to 3:00 p.m. forgetting to eat anything (except a chocolate chip cookie leftover from last night); you forget to drink water and binge on coffee and wine instead; and before you know it, you're weary and worn out.

The quickest way to burnout (and subsequent chaos) is to neglect your physical needs.

E – Empower Yourself

Once we address our physical needs, we can focus on the needs of our inner world. *Empower Yourself* is where the heart, mind, and soul are tended; where we examine our emotional, intellectual, and spiritual needs—and implement a plan to meet those needs. This might involve booking a therapy session, taking a class, finding a church or small group, or reading books.

With objective awareness of our emotional needs, on our best days, we could freely savor the goodness in our journey. On the most difficult days, we could pursue solutions to heal what hurts.

With tended hearts, sharp minds, and nourished souls, we avoid stalling out in life, laying crucial groundwork for the Life Segments to follow.

A – All Your People

With our physical and emotional needs satisfied, we can think about relationships. This may sound counterintuitive, given that women have been educated for millennia to put the needs of others ahead of their own. Our people deserve our best, but we can't offer it to them until we've first become our best selves. All of us want to do our best for our families and friends.

People are the most valuable resource on the planet, and they require special care. With a solid physical and emotional foundation, we can give these relationships the respect they deserve.

As a wife and mother, the four people closest to me are my husband and three kids. Regularly, I ask myself what I can do to care for and support them. The first two things on the list? Maintaining my physical and emotional well-being. After I've taken care of my basic needs, I can focus on making lunches, lending an ear, or helping study for a spelling test.

After I've taken care of my immediate family, I move on to my extended family and friends, team, customers, and finally my audience. Prioritizing *All My People* helps me invest in relationships that make life worthwhile.

Visualize a life where you regularly assess what your people need from you—what they need to prosper—and prioritize giving it to them.

R—Resources and Responsibilities

Our lives revolve around the three checkpoints of *Resources and Responsibilities*: home, transportation, and finances. To prevent unwanted surprises, our homes need a system for cleaning and repair; our vehicles need a maintenance schedule; and our bills, taxes, and budgets must be paid, filed, and managed.

In this Life Segment, you'll find the less glamorous parts of life. Procrastination in this area usually results in an emergency: a broken appliance, kitchen fire, flat tire, or late fee. Putting off general maintenance throws us off-balance: waiting until Tax Day to file taxes, waiting until the light is on to get the oil changed, waiting until the day of a party to shop for food. It's in these moments of emergency that we find ourselves donning our fireman's gear and sacrificing something else: sleep, a workout, time with family, or reliable transportation.

Normally, when I'm having a day where I feel like I'm coming unglued, it's because I haven't allocated my resources properly.

Disaster can usually be avoided if resources and responsibilities are properly managed. My day isn't ruined by minor mishaps if I perform a few simple tasks daily or weekly.

T—Trade and Talent

For some, *Trade and Talent* is a profession: what puts food on the table and money in the bank. For others, it's a side-hustle or artistic expression. Sometimes it's volunteer work: hours spent as a classroom aide or tending the community garden.

No matter what your work life looks like, there is a world where you feel energized and empowered to make decisions and can set boundaries and be effective with the time you have allocated—when a bad day at work doesn't ruin your week. Think about what it would feel like to be fully engaged with your job and duties and log off when you're finished.

It's tempting to bump the Trade and Talent Life Segment up on the to-do list. I still catch myself saying yes to a client, knowing it will create chaos at home during dinner. It's hard to say no, because I don't want to disappoint people! Or sometimes I'll be excited about a creative brief and dive into research on my phone instead of being present with my family. But the second we put work first, the framework fails.

Maybe it's not your work life that is out of whack. Maybe it's relational stress or a flat tire, or maybe you forget to manage your physical or emotional health. Whatever the imbalance, HEART will quickly bring us back to center.

Take a moment to consider: Which Life Segment feels the most out of balance for you?

WHERE IS THE FUN STUFF?

Am I saying you should go to a party, because it falls under *A*, before you manage your bills? Not necessarily. Whether you should attend the party hinges on the benefit you stand to derive from it. Will attendance at the party deepen important, non-toxic relationships, and have you set aside and committed time to pay your bills? Then by all means attend. But if the party won't move you forward to becoming the person you want to be, why attend? Worse yet, what if it surrounds you with people who don't encourage or positively influence you? It would be wiser to go for a walk or read a book. Ask yourself why you want to go and, more importantly, what you need right now. If the fun thing doesn't satisfy an unmet need, then you have a clear answer whether or not to attend the event.

Just as Maslow's hierarchy of needs builds from physical needs to self-actualization, so, too, do the Life Segments have an intentional order: H, E, A, R, then T. The sequential ordering of HEART establishes balance, rooting us in self-care and resulting in quality of life, joy, and real contentment.

Your physical needs come first for the reasons Maslow noted. We must care for ourselves to be in the best shape to care for our people. It's a cliché example, but put your own oxygen mask on first.

After physical needs come our emotional needs. We can't serve others if we're having an emotional meltdown or are running on empty. Addressing the needs of our inner worlds prepares us to next focus on our relationships and responsibilities.

People matter and they need to come before finances, chores, and work.

Each Life Segment acts as a building block for the next. When you prioritize self-care, you position yourself for personal growth. When you're healthy emotionally, mentally, and spiritually, you'll form deeper, more meaningful relationships.

With our relational well-being steadied, we can shift our attention to financial obligations and household duties. When we have stewarded these material responsibilities, we can ask ourselves the most meaningful question of all: How can I use my talents and skills to best serve my community and our world?

Notice how using HEART goals (especially as opposed to SMART goals) changes the way we approach organizing our lives.

HEART pulls in emotion, subsequently tying in purpose and meaning. By building on our needs, HEART prevents chaos from the beginning. By focusing on the present, instead of constantly trying to manage future results, we're free to explore our beautiful journeys. On the practical side of things, HEART prompts us to anticipate obstacles, better preparing us to overcome them, when they arise. HEART doesn't require willpower and brute force to make progress, but attends to our emotional and mental needs, fostering motivation and compelling us to action.

Traditional goal-setting usually treats the symptoms of our lives—"What is wrong with my life?"—while HEART takes a more holistic approach: "What is right, and how can we build on that?" While traditional goal-setting methods ask you to make your goals achievable and realistic, the process itself isn't flexible enough for everyday life. Most goal-setting systems don't specify what *types* of goals to set to enjoy a fulfilling life, or *how many* goals are too many. There is no instruction on how to prioritize your goals; measuring and tracking is complicated, cumbersome, and one more thing on your to-do list. Because this type of goal-setting is rooted in comparison, it doesn't account for your identity as an individual. Traditional goal-setting comes with a warning label: you might achieve what you don't want, whereas with HEART, you will get what you need—which is ultimately what your heart desires.

How to Use HEART

I use HEART in four ways:

- Long-term, big-picture planning (some people call this goal-setting).
- Monthly and weekly planning (not every week—because once you find balance you can coast for a bit). We will learn how to do this in Part III.
- Daily check-in (especially helpful when life's storms arise). When life becomes chaotic, I find it helpful to pull away and center myself by quickly walking through each letter: H, E, A, R, and T. When life gets out of control, I pause, evaluate whether I am using HEART, and start at the beginning of the acronym with my physical needs.
- A reflection tool. Using HEART in hindsight can give us an objective perspective on our actions and choices. Reflection creates personal growth, inspires change, informs our narratives, and deepens our understanding of ourselves and others.

HEART helps us identify what's going wrong in our day, week, month, or year. If I'm feeling off, I run through the Life Segments to figure out what's bothering me, and I adjust.

Whether you're using HEART for long-term visioning, weekly or monthly planning, or daily check-ins, the order remains the same.

In 2019, I was invited to speak about HEART at an entrepreneurs' workshop. I handed out workbooks, and hopped onto a cute brass barstool in a swanky co-working space. After working through the exercises, one woman raised her hand. She was pregnant, with a toddler at home, running a new business, and, I found out afterward, stressed about expenses. Work was pulling all her time and energy away from her family. Hesitantly, she asked, "What if you're in a season where you have to prioritize work first?"

I felt compassion for her as I responded, shaking my head, "It won't work." I continued on with my personal story: "Six years ago, with a young business, a stressful marriage, and financial burdens, I took two months off to spend time with my daughter when she was born. I didn't forget my work responsibilities, but I never let it pull me away from her. When I felt work tug, I maintained balance by working my HEART list in the right order. I focused on my vision to decrease work time, increase revenue, and spend more time with my family, while taking care of myself.

"As my fledgling business took off, I focused on 'quality of life decisions.' I decided I wouldn't sacrifice my own personal health or sanity or relationships for money or work. As we were putting the systems in place for the new business, this decision forced us to build margin around different operations.

"We shipped in cycles. We were selling planners, and we'd turn the cart on, sell for a week, and then turn the cart off, ship and rest for a week, then do it again."

My point was: the right choice is in many cases the counterintuitive choice. Life has a way of surprising us with solutions. We must trust the process.

But the process is messy and can often be scary.

You might think, *Sometimes things fail, right? Sometimes our goals don't work. And then what? What if you're the only breadwinner in your family, and you have to provide?*

You're right. Maybe you're in a demanding season of start-up. Stepping away from work responsibilities may feel impossible or like a sure death sentence for your career. Moving from commitments you've already made to a HEART lifestyle—which focuses on quality of life—will take practice and time.

To clarify, I'm not telling you to skip work! Prioritize your primary needs first. Make sure the baby has adequate care. Or if you're home when you work, don't take a conference call if the baby is crying. Learn how to say no. Resist the urge to sacrifice family to hustle. Set boundaries. Avoid time suckers, coffee dates with people who want to "pick your brain." Don't pull all-nighters. Don't sacrifice your health. Refuse to compare yourself to others. Celebrate what you *have* accomplished and give yourself grace where you haven't met up with your hopes and expectations.

Also, think of what's at stake if you *don't* stop and refocus: your kid's first goal at a soccer game, your daughter's sixth birthday, healing laughter over dinner with friends, and your own mental, emotional, and physical health. You can be selective about what you commit to, but if you let work and career or the desire for more stuff or money overtake your life, these are the prices you will pay.

When we prioritize our needs in order of importance, everything else balances out. If we reverse or mess with the order, we cannot expect the same results. The order matters. You can't prioritize Trade and Talent first, then Resources and Responsibilities, and then Help Yourself. Work won't *work* if you've neglected your basic needs. And in the most counterintuitive way, work will work itself out if you take a small amount of your time to focus on what matters most.

I'll coach you through identifying your needs in each Life Segment (part II) and how to use HEART (part III) soon. For now, get to know the many ways HEART orients your life and gets you back on track toward what matters.

Adaptable and Fit to You

Goals—SMART or not—are no substitute for a life management system. And we need a life management system. Our lives are spinning faster than ever before—while throwing us a fair share of curveballs, restarts, and do-overs.

Screaming babies, the passing of a friend, an unexpected hospital visit, fatigue.

PMS, a kid's forgotten homework.

Local crises, national crises, natural disasters, or the occasional parking ticket.

This is the stuff traditional goal-setting does not take into account. It's impossible to anticipate all the trappings a year will throw at us 365 days in advance. If we mapped out every appointment for our entire year on January 1, can you imagine the mess our planners would be? I'm all for messy planners, but the cross-outs, strike-throughs, and paper smudges from erasing so many times would drive me crazy.

HEART takes real life into account in two ways:

One, there are no deadlines. You can assign a deadline to a desire; you can't assign a deadline to a need. If you miss a deadline or your life gets chaotic (which, spoiler, it will), you simply give yourself grace and start again. Each Life Segment is a continual process, in constant improvement.

Second, as surprises interrupt your day or life, specific tasks can shift, but the basic need categories remain the same. Because HEART centers on the categories, the tasks within those segments can adapt to every situation.

Imbalance can befall us in any season. A young mother with an infant is sacrificing sleep, and exercise, but she can focus on nutrition and water. A project at work, an unexpected health crisis, a book deadline (*ahem*) can all throw our focus off of our HEART priorities. Taking care of an elderly parent can be demanding on a normal sleep and exercise schedule, but you can take small steps to care for yourself, and those small steps will contribute to helping you maintain as much balance in life as possible.

When we address our needs we address the root of stress and comparison.

And because HEART is needs-based, it fits uniquely into your life, so you won't end up with arbitrary goals.

Going back to our needs helps us meet ourselves where we are. If you haven't had enough sleep, HEART prompts you to remedy that. If you have five kids or no kids, your relational needs change accordingly. If you work full-time or part-time or at your own discretion, your needs will meet you there. Instead of picking an achievement from another person's life and superimposing it onto yours, look at your needs. Your needs will always direct you to ambitions that highlight your abilities, minimize your limitations, and maximize your strengths.

We know what makes life beautiful: the love, joy, and goodness we feel from day to day. The way we experience those emotions is directly tied to how well we address our needs. Because HEART is based on your needs, your efforts will automatically help you move toward that beautiful life.

Write It Down, Make It Beautiful

1. What would it look like to stop asking what you want and ask what you need?
2. Where have you been ignoring your needs?
3. How is neglecting your needs affecting other areas of your life?
4. What is one thing you know you need right now?
5. What Life Segment does this represent?
6. What steps could you take to meet that need?

Chapter 3

"IT'S LIKE RIDING A BIKE!"

*"Life is like riding a bicycle. To keep your
balance, you must keep moving."*
ALBERT EINSTEIN

In 2015, my husband, David, and I moved from Oklahoma City to a town in the middle of nowhere. When we arrived, our kids were five, four, and two. Since the community was walkable, we thought about buying a golf cart; however, one of the reasons we justified moving was to live a healthier lifestyle—and owning a golf cart seemed like the antithesis of that.

So, we bought bikes.

If you've never taught a kid to ride a bike, you should. It demands patience. If I coached math homework with the same fortitude and encouragement required to coach bike riding, the total number of tears and headaches would be drastically lower.

At first, my kids wouldn't even entertain the idea of getting on their new bikes. I tried demonstrating, but that didn't change their minds. I could see the skepticism in their faces: they couldn't see how they were the kind of kids who biked.

That was until they saw our seven-year-old neighbor sailing down the street one day. Suddenly, they were willing to try.

It didn't go well at first. First attempts are never perfect. They wobbled all over the place, panicking and fearful. Five seconds of balance, and they'd sort of tip over into the grass beside the sidewalk.

I was watching, though. I noticed my kids were keeping their eyes on the pedals and the handlebars. They were looking down, instead of where they wanted to go. I realized that if they would quit focusing on their feet and start looking ahead, at the horizon, they would find their balance. "Look at the flag! The flag! The flag!" I yelled after them, and as soon as they passed the flag, I'd scream, "Look at the rosebush! The rosebush! The rosebush!"

It was a riot.

"And don't forget to pedal!" I hollered as they looked up and out, because if they didn't stay in action, they'd fall over again. Poor things. I tried so hard not to laugh.

The whole experience was a light-bulb moment, verified by Einstein himself. Life is like riding a bike. To balance that bike, life requires three things: vision, focus, and action.

My kids needed vision. And so do we. We must visualize ourselves as successful bike riders, life livers, dream chasers (or whatever thing it is we're valiantly trying to do).

My kids also needed focus. We steer where we look. If we look at the flag or the rosebush or the next bend in the road, that's where the bike takes us. Any attempt to see over the horizon will lead us to the ditch.

And lastly, my kids needed to stay in action. We need to keep moving. If we stop pedaling, not only will we stop making progress on our journey but we will lose our balance.

When they got the hang of it, it was glorious to see the wind ruffling their hair, the sparkle of freedom in their eyes, the exhilaration on their faces as they experienced that first magical taste of independent flight. Goal achieved.

The three keys to riding a bike are not just the three keys to balance for a four-year-old. They are the keys to riding through a beautiful and balanced life. The HEART framework is designed to help you get there. But if I taught you HEART without discussing this first, there's a high likelihood you'd do what my kids did when they first saw those bikes: run the other direction.

You wouldn't even use the framework (action) because you wouldn't see yourself as the kind of person who has a beautiful, balanced life (vision).

That said, with this trio in mind—vision, focus, and action—you will not only understand HEART, you'll see for yourself the way I saw my daughter the day she learned to ride a bike: soaring down a sidewalk, enjoying every second of this beautiful, messy gift called life.

This Is Your Brain on Change

If riding through life is meant to be enjoyable, why does it feel so *hard*? It's a fair question and it has to do with the term *self-sabotage.*

Sabotage is the deliberate destruction or weakening of something, usually covertly.[1] Self-sabotage is when the subconscious mind (that stress eats chocolate) clashes with the rational, conscious mind (that wants to eat salad and exercise). This is when you want to do something—like create a beautiful life, for example—but then act out behaviors that create the opposite reality.[2]

We all struggle with self-sabotage at times, because it works—at least, in the short-term. The term I learned in therapy for this is *medicating*: using a distraction to avoid dealing with emotional pain or something else we don't want to face. Turning to your phone, food, and alcohol are all easy ways to avoid feeling the hardship and adversity.

But short-term advantages aside, self-defeating behavior always conflicts with a deeper sense of peace, meaning, and contentment.

The magical trio—vision, focus, and action—is our first defense against the innate tendency to self-destruct. It's reassuring to know what to expect, even if it is all downhill. The certainty of chaos, frustration, and despair can comfort us, oddly enough. The thought of change, let alone the miserable gauntlet of transition, can terrify us more than our current circumstances.

Instead of allowing things to change, we dig our heels in—we sabotage. This is why I like to think of sabotage less as *self-sabotage* and more as *change-sabotage*. We often extinguish the sparks of opportunity life presents. We've become pretty cozy in a controlled world that could slip from our change-resistant fingertips. Instead of allowing things to change us, when we read a book like this or learn about something like HEART that could improve our lives, we think *oh yeah, nice idea . . . sounds cool . . .* and then we go back to staring at meaningless things on our phone.

Change is hard. It's even harder when we lack a vision and self-image of who we could become, when we're distracted by comparison and shiny things and allow ourselves to become emotionally demotivated and inactive.

Most self-sabotage can be overcome. Some people can do this by sheer force of will. The rest of us, however, would like an easier way.

Whether you find it easy or challenging to resist your natural tendency for self-sabotage, the first step is to become aware of the signs and identify those that apply to you personally.

Emotional Eating. Have you ever stress eaten your feelings? It's too easy to turn to empty calories or alcohol to cope with stress and worry. Food with little nutritional value works in the short run: it makes us feel better and distracts us from what hurts. This behavior undermines values like eating a healthy diet and becoming your best physical self.

Procrastination. You put off a workout for another Netflix episode, swap writing reports for office cleaning, or delay scheduling that dentist appointment. We all procrastinate from time to time. When these actions become habitual behaviors with substantial negative consequences, it's time to inspect.

Tardiness. Maybe you're habitually late. You want to be productive and effective with your time, so you overestimate your abilities. Intentions may be good, but being late erodes relationships and undermines trust and respect among friends and family.

Commitment Issues. You might struggle with emotional sensitivity and fear of being harmed. Though you want to develop meaningful connections, you destroy your relationships out of the desire to alleviate anxiety.

Freezing. You may slow to a stop while attempting to accomplish your objectives. You have the ability and desire to succeed, and a fantastic opportunity, yet something holds you back. You might forget a deadline or fail to prepare a presentation. Perhaps you start projects but never complete them. Maybe you fantasize about accomplishing something of tremendous personal importance but never act on it. You give up before you even start.

Perfectionism. The root of perfectionism is the desire to protect ourselves from failure. Perfectionism is another form of procrastination: the impulse to continuously work on a project is a veiled attempt to avoid criticism.

Overworking. All-time favorite. Scared of too much change? I'll just create a bunch of chaos by picking up a few extra tasks at work.

Staring at Your Phone. Do you catch yourself missing out on conversations, important moments with friends, or even big events with your kids because you were staring at something mind-numbing on Instagram? You're not alone. Apps are the primary culprits of this (they're good at draining our battery and our attention), but consider that this may be a coping mechanism to avoid change.

Rather than beat yourself up about any of this (which is easy) maybe you can see this as a way you're protecting yourself by preventing *too much* change.

It's not just self-defeating behaviors that keep us from a beautiful life. It's also self-defeating thoughts. Psychologist and author Robert Firestone calls this the critical inner voice. The critical inner voice is a cruel antiself that has turned against us. These thoughts question our abilities, tell us we are undeserving, and make us paranoid and suspicious of ourselves and those close to us.[3]

This vein of thinking makes it nearly impossible for us to change our self-image.

Listen for the hurt and fear behind the critical inner voice in the following all-too-familiar statements:

- People will judge me if I fail. People will be jealous if I succeed.
- Don't raise your hand to ask that question. People might laugh at you and label you as incompetent.
- People can't laugh at me. If people laugh at me and think I'm incompetent, I'll lose my confidence, status, and sanity.
- If I express confidence in my gifts, they'll label me a liar.

- Starting something new is too risky, and I can't predict the exact outcome. I'd better back off.
- If I succeed, I'll get a new set of responsibilities. What if I don't have what it takes?

Our critical inner voice develops in response to our early life experiences.

Children will absorb negative ideas about themselves from their parents or early caregivers. Someone who felt abandoned as a child might develop insecurity in adult relationships. The inner critic feeds a self-fulfilling prophecy: *How can you trust him? He will leave you. Be cautious and avoid getting too close.*

Someone who had an overpowering or intrusive parent may feel smothered by attention in relationships. She may hear voices saying, *He's too clingy. Can't he leave you alone? You'll be fine on your own. You can't stand being so close.*

For someone whose parents viewed them as lazy, they may grow up feeling worthless. When that person puts less effort into their work, their idea of themselves becomes a reality.

Someone who grew up with a self-hating parent who identified themselves as weak or a failure might develop similar self-destructive views about himself. If our parents were insecure about their looks, we might adopt similar anxieties without recognizing them. In social or public settings, we may feel self-conscious and unsure of ourselves. If we watched our parents struggle with insufficient confidence, we may find ourselves hypercritical of others, because that's the only way we understand self-esteem to work.

Growing up, the words we hear influence us, leading to lifelong negative self-talk patterns. We tend to repeat unpleasant, outdated behavior patterns in relationships. Even if we *think* a different ending is possible, our subconscious brain doesn't *believe* it. We sabotage ourselves by giving free rein to our critical inner voices.

But it's not always childhood that forms the critical inner voice. Later life trauma—both big *T* trauma and little *t* trauma[4]—can affect us at a deep level. Either one will shape us.

We can't go back in time. As adults, however, we can choose to identify the self-defeating thoughts and beliefs we absorbed as children and young adults and intentionally choose to defy programmed behaviors.

Welcome to Your Brain

To understand why change is so difficult, we need to understand the rudimentary mechanics of the human brain, how our values and beliefs drive us, and how emotions are our best motivators. And on that note, I'd like to introduce you to some lizards.

If you have to read several paragraphs on how the brain works, I thought I'd try to make it fun. Come with me, if you will, on a Whitney's-imagination-inspired journey into the brain.

Let's start at the top, in the control room, otherwise known as the prefrontal cortex. Note the uniformed crew sitting in front of the big window, in front of a dashboard filled with buttons, clocks, and graphs of information coming in from the rest of the brain. That guy standing over there with the clipboard appears to be the captain; his gestures and commands indicate he regulates the functions happening here. Second in command, a lady, stands behind him, and they balance each other out: one strict, logical, calculating; the other kind, helpful, social, emotional.

It's hectic here; this squad has many responsibilities. They're keeping you on time, managing your schedule, reminding you about your to-do list, and helping you rationalize the 35,000 decisions you make on any given day.[5]

A new door opens to the hippocampus—a room that looks like part library, part art gallery. A librarian is working behind the desk. The shelves are labeled. One says "long-term memory." One says "frequently accessed." The boxes on the shelves are labeled as well. This is the preconscious mind. As you spend a few moments admiring the beauty of this space, you notice that the crew from the control room occasionally pops down to retrieve a file, and then disappears back upstairs.

Dropping one floor, the doors open onto an industrial scene. This feels, and looks, like a factory. Conveyor belts and gears and equipment transfer boxes back and forth. There's not a crew member in sight. Instead, lizards, each creatively uniformed, shuffle boxes around. Capers are obviously afoot, and the vibe is fast and haphazard. This is what I wanted to show you. It's the limbic brain, also known as the *amygdala*.

The amygdala is an essential part of the brain: a neurological foundation. Its job is to respond to fearful situations by prompting us to respond—*fight, flight, freeze, fawn*.[6] The amygdala is good at saving our lives, but it's bad (like, very bad) at helping you create a beautiful one.

The amygdala is casually called the lizard brain—hence my imagination populating this part of the brain with purple reptiles. We rely on the amygdala for survival, so the lizard brain is geared to sense danger. If we stand here long enough, we'll see the crew of lizards respond, instinctively, to the situations only the control room has eyes on; there are no windows here—just incoming data, fed to this crew by the control room upstairs.

The lizard crew has one major flaw: they're terrible communicators. When a memo arrives from the control room/neocortex, they don't look at it unless it has a picture. Can you imagine being the commander, trying to give the lizards some direction, and the only way they'll listen to you is if you draw stick figures? To the lizards, an image is truly worth a thousand words. I'm convinced that images are the language of our limbic brain.

They're not the brightest, but the lizards play a role equally as important as the prefrontal cortex crew. We *need* our amygdala. The prefrontal cortex crew uses logic and data to inform decisions, unlike the lizards who operate on instinct. And very often, the lizards are right. The subconscious knows more than we give it credit for.

Understanding how these seemingly oppositional parts of our brains function gives us an advantage to create change in our lives.

The lizards help us survive, but as I said before, survival does not equate to a beautiful life. When we're trying to change to become more of our best selves, that change (no matter how healthy or good) may trigger alarm bells. And when that happens, we go right back to the way things were before—even when those things weren't good for us.

The answer is to learn, at times, to override that primal fear response so that we can create the beautiful, peaceful life we know is possible. But, of course, this begs the question: how?

From the Head Back to the HEART

It's been said that the longest journey is from your head to your heart. Understanding how our head works is foundational to knowing how to use HEART to help us find our way back to meaningful ambitions, confident balance, and beautiful living.

Our brains do many things for us, but without HEART, they can keep us stuck in self-destructive patterns (those pesky lizards). A new way forward is through that magical trio that taught my kids how to ride a bike: vision, focus, and action.

Vision

And I mean, actual vision. Images in your mind, spoken in the only language the lizards understand: pictures. The framework you'll learn in the chapters that follow will help you create a vision for yourself and your life that goes beyond arbitrary goal-setting. This has less to do with what you want to accomplish and more to do with *how you see yourself.* Remember the story of Nehemiah? Creating vision starts with seeing clearly where you are, knowing where you need to be, and recognizing the gap between the two.

Vision has to do with how you see yourself as a person. Are you the kind of person who rides a bike? For my kids, they became that when they saw the seven-year-old neighbor ride his bike. Sometimes that's all it takes: envisioning yourself in action to communicate to the lizards that it's possible. Before seeing the possibility, my kids couldn't visualize themselves as cyclists. But when they saw our neighbor do it, something clicked. *Maybe we could be the kind of kids who ride bikes,* they thought. And they set to work trying.

Keep this bike analogy at the front of your mind. When you hear your critical inner voice telling you that you aren't the kind of person who is organized or goes to bed early or who gets things done in time, think about my kids watching that seven-year-old ride his bike. Maybe you could be the kind of person who does all of those things, if you envision it.

Focus

When you hear me say "if you envision it" I don't want you to interpret that as: *she's saying I haven't already worked at this.* I know you work at it. Impossibly hard. Knowing what a hard worker you are, what if success in this area isn't about working harder but about focusing the hard work you've already done on the *right things*?

Think about my kids staring at their pedals or at the ground and crashing every time. Their success in riding a bike wasn't about them pedaling harder or faster but about lifting up their heads and focusing on the right things. I pray that, as you read this book, your focus will shift to the right things—the things that will make a tangible difference in your life. What I know is that HEART does this. It changes our focus.

Action

We all know things don't change unless we act. But have you ever felt like you were frantically taking action, only to make your situation worse than it was to begin with? Going back to HEART helps us know what next steps to take, in keeping with our vision.

A MORE BEAUTIFUL LIFE

A new endeavor is exciting until it becomes uncontrollable and chaotic, and we can't stop or swerve out of the way. That sense of life spinning out of control causes us to slam the brakes and impede progress.

When this starts to happen, it's time to rescue our initial energy and enthusiasm, that vision of ourselves as *someone who rides a bike*. I hope that, when the speed picks up and you're finally making progress, rather than being immobilized by anxiety, you'll feel as liberated and delighted as my daughter appeared to me that day.

Our brains are a force to be reckoned with: they hold a wealth of information and work tirelessly to keep us safe. However, they have the potential to prevent us from achieving what we truly desire: transformation! You may change established patterns by reflecting, being aware, being purposeful, and being gentle with yourself. And if you do, you'll become more than a cyclist. You'll be the one gliding through town in style, inspiring your neighbors to follow suit.

How will you get there? By starting with HEART.

Write It Down, Make It Beautiful

1. Big picture, what's your vision for your life?
2. What obstacles stand in your way, and how can you focus on the solution, rather than the obstacle?
3. Where could you take action? What do you think the next steps could be? Park them here. You may or may not come back to the list on this page. The important part of this exercise is in letting go of anything that might unknowingly be holding you back. We need a clean slate with plenty of blank space for designing a beautiful life.

PART II

Chapter 4

H–HELP YOURSELF

> "We have all a better guide in ourselves, if we would
> attend to it, than any other person can be."
> JANE AUSTEN[1]

A typical morning around our house is, in one word, *loud*. As David gets ready and the kids scramble to find school uniforms, I make a beeline for the coffee maker. At least twelve times over, I'll hear someone yell across the house, "Where's [fill in the blank with a thing they're responsible for tracking]?" I hear battles over breakfast and kids bossing kids as backpacks clatter through halls. It's a racket.

While the kids are concerned about who is riding shotgun, who has stepped on their toes, or recounting what saga they'll tell their friends at school, David and I are thinking about the responsibilities and obligations that await us after school drop-off.

On my best days, even amid this chaos, I'm already making choices using HEART. Coffee may be in hand, but the water bottle is right beside it. The decision on lunch is already made. My walking shoes are on and tied, and I'm moving through the house, picking up laundry, starting a load, closing drawers, and wiping off counters.

Of course, that's not every day.

There are bad mornings too. If I didn't sleep well the night before or go to bed at a decent hour, the day starts off on the wrong foot. And it only takes one wrong-foot-start for the chaos of the mornings to get the best of me—of any of us. If work yesterday was hectic, I struggle with the temptation to glance at my email. If I'm feeling the pressure of a deadline, I'm more likely to snap at someone, create a false sense of urgency, and drag them down with me.

Those days are my worst days. I'm not proud of them, but I have them. And on those days, when the kids are finally out the door, I still haven't paid attention to anything related to my physical body. My teeth aren't brushed, my face isn't washed, and I haven't even *thought* of exercise.

Not the healthiest start to the day.

We wear many hats—mom, wife, daughter, sister, employee, entrepreneur, teacher, coach, or small group leader. We wake up to lists of projects, tasks, and people to care for other than ourselves. Without careful planning, our physical health ends up at the bottom of our priority list. The gym? That can wait. Twenty minutes on the bike? Who has time? Plan a nutritious meal? I can't even.

It's these days that feel like a lost cause—before they even begin. I survive on cheese (oh, cheese), crackers, or fast food. I follow my coffee with an energy drink to ward off the urge to nap. Unsuccessful, I nap instead of taking a walk around the block. Soon enough, the day is over, and I haven't given a thought to the four checkpoints of helping myself: sleep, water, nutrition, and movement.

We all value our physical health. But on a chaotic, unbalanced day, we can often push our bodies to the back burner. We start with coffee and end with wine. Making that dentist appointment falls off the to-do list. We care for the next thing nagging instead of ourselves. Then, we wonder why we are exhausted, sore, and in a terrible mood—stuck in a grind and snappy with the people we love.

Why We Neglect Our Physical Needs

When confronted with a long to-do list, taking care of our physical well-being doesn't always seem urgent or vital. We have so many daily responsibilities and—for many of us—a job on top of it all.

And then, there are the fires: minor mishaps calling for our attention. Maybe it's a broken appliance, a text from your boss asking you to cover a shift, or a friend calling you in tears.

Just writing this brings back that tight feeling in my chest. I feel the anxiety building as I tighten my jaw. And we haven't even addressed our availability to *our people.*

We all neglect our physical well-being at times. Every woman I know has put her own needs aside to care for others. And willingly! It doesn't always feel like a sacrifice. I find joy in caring for those around me! Skipping a workout or finding an easy snack can seem like the right, practical thing to do in the spirit of meeting others' needs.

But what happens when we repeatedly focus on meeting the urgent demands of loved ones before satisfying *our* basic needs?

Reinforced by the subtle conditioning of advertising, media, culture, and religion, we believe caring for others means putting their needs ahead of our own. We sacrifice for our kids, partners, family, and friends—we stay up late and wake up early, believing we must put our own needs last to prove our love. And many of us wear this devotion like a badge of honor. We're sick, tired, and proud of it.

Ever been there? Or seen someone who is?

What is misleading us? You might think: *Isn't my career consequential? Isn't having an income more important than a healthy breakfast? Aren't my relationships more important than exercise? Doesn't my family, my community, deserve my attention?*

If you find yourself saying anything like this, you're not wrong. Your marriage *is* more important than a twenty-minute jog . . . in the long run. Your children's education *is* more important than how many liters of water you drink on a particular day . . . in the long run. Your career *is* more important than your meal-prep routine . . . in the long run.

But a kind word to a spouse takes two seconds.

Your kids are watching your example of self-care.

A nutritious meal-plan fuels your mind and career.

The unglamorous daily duties don't warrant an epitaph. Not many people lay on their deathbed saying, "Wow, I'm so glad I drank so much water." We don't.

The *H* is at the base of the pyramid because meeting your basic physical needs is foundational. Without a concerted, intentional focus on your physical well-being, everything else will eventually crumble.

If you devoted your time to personal well-being first, you'd be a much better firefighter for your people. How do you best care for others if you're not feeling and functioning at your best? If your mind is clouded by sleepiness or distraction?

You can't.

While other elements of your life may be more vital in the long term, your bodily requirements must be satisfied first.

Helping Yourself: Need 1

The *H* of HEART stands for *Help Yourself*. And when I say *Help Yourself*, I'm referring to your physical health.

Maslow emphasized that safety and basic physical needs come first. You must eat to survive. You must have access to (and drink) clean water. You must shelter from the elements: heat and cold. Your physical well-being is a prerequisite for doing anything else.

Think about when you catch a cold. When I come down with something, I can't think about anything else but getting better. If I do press on without taking proper care of myself, my work and relationships suffer for it. I am not my best self. I am not at the top of my game. Without your physical needs met, you will not function. One cannot move forward to care for people and relationships or giving back when food, shelter, or health are an issue.

I can't be present for my family if I'm exhausted. If I don't have time to eat well or exercise, I can't serve my team or my family, and everyone feels the impact. And what are the long-term impacts to my career, my ability to earn income, if I don't have the time to care for myself?

You might say to me, "Well, Whitney, I can't ignore these other parts of my life—my job or my marriage—they'll fall apart!" Yes, but they will also fall apart if you neglect this part of your life: your physical needs.

After months or even years of neglecting our physical needs, this area may require extra attention. But the more we listen to our bodies' needs, the easier it will be to automate our routines. Self-care is easy and simple, and sets us up to thrive. We will achieve more and be more physically, mentally, and emotionally present if we take care of our bodies.

SELF-CARE VS. SELF-INDULGENCE

When we talk about taking care of our bodies, we must carefully distinguish between self-care and self-indulgence. Self-care is meal prep for a nutritious week ahead; self-indulgence is gorging on unhealthy foods. Self-care is proper hygiene and appearance maintenance; self-indulgence is a spa day on the credit card that leads you deeper into debt. Self-care prioritizes time off to recharge and renew through workouts, meditations, or therapy; self-indulgence is taking a personal day simply because I don't want to work.

The difference is in our motives: self-care makes us better for the people we serve; self-indulgence ignores the needs of those around us. The benefits of self-care are long-term: positive relationships, long-lasting health. The benefits of self-indulgence are temporary, if not detrimental overall. There is a fine line between the two, but we must understand it. Prioritizing our needs for physical well-being is the cornerstone for all other areas of life. To neglect the physical self is the surest way to sabotage our potential. It's the surefire way to set ourselves on a crash course.

The four checkpoints of *Help Yourself* can improve your physical health: sleep, water, nutrition, and movement. It's not rocket science, but focusing on these tiny categories can bring remarkable healing and peace to your life. As you read, ask yourself how often you neglect these checkpoints? What advantages are you missing out on?

Sleep

Without sleep, our bodies shut down.

Sleep is our first line of defense. It strengthens our immune systems,[2] helps us focus,[3] and enhances our productivity throughout the day.[4] Insufficient sleep is linked to weight gain,[5] hypertension,[6] stress,[7] inflammation,[8] diabetes,[9] and heart disease.[10] Without it, we simply cannot function.

If you want to know how true this is, talk to a new mom. There's a reason sleep deprivation is used as torture treatment in POW camps. It makes the deprived person feel as if they're dying a slow, painful death.

New parents aside, most people aren't this sleep deprived. Here and there, they cut corners. *Six hours should be enough; I'll stay up to check email and get some laundry done.* The temptation to push yourself is relentless because the to-do list is relentless. But the trade-off isn't worth it.

Staying up another hour to finish the laundry is more detrimental than getting up an hour early and tackling tasks with renewed energy, even if you're a night owl. Think about this: What if we attacked every day fully rested? Would you feel better if you always got enough sleep? (Sidenote: for those with very young kids, give yourself all the grace. If you know someone with very young kids, send a lasagna.)

You don't have to track your sleep patterns to ensure you're getting enough sleep. We can ask ourselves a few questions, and if our answers are honest, they will guide us.

- How many hours of sleep is optimal for you?
- What time do you need to go to sleep?

- What wakes you up in the middle of the night? What do you need to do so those disruptions don't continue to happen?
- What temperature, bedding, and light do you need to sleep well?
- What helps you fall asleep?
- When do you feel most rested?
- Do you need to limit screen time at night?
- Do you need a nighttime routine?
- Do you need to avoid scheduling appointments before a specific time in the morning?
- Do you need to eliminate alcohol?

Getting good sleep has been a struggle for me for years. It wasn't until I prioritized sleep that I discovered how much better I could function. Historically, I'm a night owl. As an introvert, my energy goes up as our house quiets down. This can make it hard to fall asleep. But as I've learned how to rest and to sleep well, I've been amazed at how my energy level stays up and balanced throughout the day.

You don't have to track your sleep patterns, but if you want to nerd out, some gadgets can tell you how many hours you need to feel rested. If you're not into statistics and graphs, prioritize getting the amount of rest you need to be your best.

Water

We know water is essential. But I didn't realize until recently how many of my body's basic functions depend on it. Water keeps everything moving. It protects our bones,[11] joints, and body temperature.[12] Not surprisingly, drinking enough water keeps us alert[13] and contented.[14]

But knowing we need water doesn't make us drink it. How can a person in the first world and the twenty-first century have near-constant access to clean drinking water and still choose not to drink it as often as she should?

Can you make it a habit? Can you set a reminder? If you're a planner, write it down: every day, drink *x* amount of water.

Filling one water bottle in the morning and drinking it at a specific time works. If I bring a glass of water to bed, I'm more likely to drink it if I wake up thirsty.

Find a creative solution if you're reluctant. Add fruit, flavoring, fizzies, or ice. Schedule it, habit-stack it, or force it. Whatever you do, do what it takes to get your H_2O. Hack it however you like, but water is priority number two.

Nutrition

Nutrition: the process of getting the vitamins, minerals, proteins, and other nutrients to keep your body healthy and thriving.

You know the telltale signs you're not getting the nutrition your body needs: lack of energy, cravings at odd hours, headaches, tummy aches.

The number one way I help myself keep a healthy diet is to create a meal plan for the week. Meal planning lays a foundation for the week ahead and takes the guesswork out of creating healthy options. There are no last-minute decisions on what to eat. There's no arguing: you and everyone else in the house know what's on the menu. I know our family's nutrition has been neglected if my kids come in hungry and ask what the plan is or if David offers to start dinner but can't find anything to thaw.

But with a plan, meals run smoothly, without too much effort, and with no last-minute stress. I pick out simple recipes, then make a grocery list. From a grocery list, I can easily order or shop for groceries. From groceries, I can prepare meals over the weekend. And if the meal prep is done, the decisions are made. All we need is someone to cook it—we'll fight over that one later.

I regularly choose simple meals: spaghetti, chili, and baked chicken. My mom taught me these skills in the kitchen, and I'm instructing my kids. I teach them how to use a slow cooker, make a roast, ribs, or shredded chicken. If I write out kid-friendly recipes for seven days a week and make sure everything is cut and ready to go, the kids can almost make their own dinner.

See? Checking the box on nutrition and teaching my kids how to cook and prioritize health, all at the same time. #momwin

If you're not a meal prep person, I encourage you to find a way to make choosing health simple. Some ideas:

- Get rid of the snack basket or fill it with healthy snacks.
- Make grocery trips when you're full and rested.
- See if you can trade off planning meals with a partner or with friends.
- Research the healthy takeout options nearest you.
- Explore meal delivery services.

The point is, you need a plan. It doesn't need to be a meal plan. But without strategies, it's too easy to reach for the convenient foods full of empty calories and no nutrients. It's too easy to put off dinner decisions, resulting in terrible takeout or frozen meals that leave you hungry an hour later.

There's nothing inherently shameful about ordering takeout or opening the freezer for dinner. But what you're putting inside your body matters because it's fueling you. Can you improve your fueling strategy?

For some of us, this might take more work. Each body is unique. Our bodies respond well or poorly to specific foods. Maybe you have food allergies. Finding out what it is in your diet that contributes to how you're feeling (whether good or bad) might take some investigating and experimentation. Finding out what makes your body feel energized might take some research and education. You might even consider talking to a nutritionist. But it's worth the effort. Your body will thank you.

Movement

Don't worry. This isn't where I make you feel guilty for not hitting the gym. Exercise is fine—but we won't address heavy training here.

Movement, however, is priceless for your health.

Movement improves your mood, releases endorphins, and gives you energy for hours.[15] Regularly moving your body will keep you alive and kicking well into old age.

We know this instinctively. Movement and exercise make us feel good and improve our day. We know we feel better about ourselves when we feel healthy. Science supports body, mind, and self-esteem benefits.[16]

My best advice for moving your body is simple: start with something feasible. Better yet, start with something fun. Take a stroll in the park with your family. Hang with the cute mall-walkers. Participate in a swimming lesson with the children at a community pool.

You don't have to be a triathlete. Do what you can, but commit to make it easier on yourself. Lay out your activewear the night before. Schedule exercising with a friend. Walk around the block instead of driving to the gym.

If *exercise* sounds daunting, don't even use the word. Dance parties, running through sprinklers, and vacuuming all count.

What prevents you from moving your body? Dread? Embarrassment? General distaste for sweat and public showers? (Raised my hand on that one.)

Don't overthink this. Overcomplicating anything is a waste of time and energy.

Here is a list of unconventional ways to move our bodies:

- Dance party in the kitchen while you're making dinner!
- Race to clean the house with the kids.
- Stretch while you're on the floor with your baby or toddler.
- Meet a friend and walk to a coffee shop.
- Borrow a toddler and try a yoga video.
- Find a cycle, barre, or mommy and me exercise class.
- Park at the far end of the store lot.
- Choose the stairs instead of the elevator or escalator.
- Pace around your office or house while having phone conversations.
- Try stretching in the mornings, evenings, or on work breaks.

I'm not a couch potato and you're not a slacker. Let's capture the thoughts (excuses) holding us back and listen to our bodies. You may feel drained, but your body is signaling for a change! Stop thinking exercise is work, and start realizing movement is fuel.

To have the courage to act, we need motivation and empathy. And remember, you don't need to run a marathon or hit a personal record to experience the benefits of moving. Wander around the block. Do jumping jacks. Pull up a yoga tutorial. There is no need to complicate movement.

I'll say it again: don't overthink this. As much as we need to hear it, we already know this truth: ignoring our bodies doesn't do us any good. As you move through *Help Yourself*, you'll find yourself hooked on the benefit (and fun) of true, authentic movement.

Your Brain on Fear

When your brain is afraid, you're bound to self-sabotage. The lizard brain, programmed to sense danger, is easily alarmed by changes, threats, and obstacles.

That's why I'm reminding you. Because while you're attempting to change for the better, your reptile brain will send you fear signals.

Even if change is as simple as drinking more water or getting out for a walk before you check your email—your lizard brain will perceive any shift in routine or habit as a threat. When this happens, you're likely to self-sabotage. This is when you catch yourself avoiding the one thing that would make you feel better, short-circuiting your brilliant plan, and chugging a third cup of coffee instead of hydrating.

Still, as logical creatures, we must learn when and how to disregard the lizards. Your greatest tool for disregarding the amygdala is awareness. Simply knowing your brain is reacting to a perceived threat can be enough to help you soothe yourself and continue forward, caring for your physical needs.

The Consequences of Not Helping Yourself

A few years ago, I was drowning in chores and appointments. One Tuesday, I was interrogated about dinner at least fifteen times before three o'clock. Truth was, I was in the middle of writing

Have you ever had a gut feeling—you knew something would or would not work out? Or a pain that only presents itself when you're stressed? Or maybe you've noticed when you get scared (for me, heights!), fear hits you in a specific place on your body (my stomach). These sensations illustrate how our bodies, thoughts, and emotions are connected. They inform one another.

It is common for our bodies to tell us what we're feeling or thinking before we're aware enough to name the emotion or articulate the thought. We grind our teeth when stressed at work or experience shoulder pain when in conflict with a friend. Headaches, stomach pain, fatigue. This is our bodies trying to tell us something.

The great news is we can use our bodies as diagnostic tools for how we're doing emotionally. Rather than immediately treating a headache with an aspirin (although do treat it eventually), we can ask ourselves, *What is causing this headache? Am I stressed? Overwhelmed? Dehydrated?*

The more we pay attention to our physical cues, the better we can address our emotions as they come up. The next time you notice something happening physically, ask yourself, *What's going on beneath the surface?*

an email, wasn't hungry, and hadn't thought about it. The moment felt like a breaking point, and, overwhelmed, I launched straight into negative self-talk: *Good grief, can't you get organized enough to cook dinner for your family?*

I meal-prep on Sundays but realized I hadn't done it this week. In the middle of making my grocery list, a friend called—and I knew she was going through a tough spot. I let it ring twice before deciding I needed to pick it up, and my meal planning could wait thirty minutes. The problem was, I didn't return to it. Instead, I picked my daughter up from a friend's house, made us a snack, and sat down to send a few work emails. Meal plan, forgotten.

This choice, however, had an unintended consequence. Because I didn't meal plan, I didn't know what to pick up at the store. Without a grocery list, I lacked initiative and procrastinated going to the store until Monday, when we were out of food. Because we didn't have lunch food on hand, I was hangry with my shopping cart, and bought impulsively. Because I was making choices on the fly, I bought what I wanted and didn't purchase everything we needed for the week. By Wednesday, we were ready for a fresh meal and bloated on junk food.

So I did what I do and regrouped with HEART.

Whenever I find myself at the bottom of a spiral like this, my body gives me physical cues—the way my stomach feels, the tension in my jaw and shoulders, or a bad headache. My response is not always physical, though. Sometimes I dispel the negative energy by snapping at David or the kids, griping about an offense, or numbing myself in front of a screen.

This is where HEART comes in handy. As I recognize these signs, I can start at the top of the acronym and work through the Life Segments.

Help Myself: How's My Sleep? Water? Nutrition? Movement?

Drinking a glass of water, eating a salad, exercising, and setting an alarm for bedtime are all things I can do to improve my day in the answers to just four questions. Circumstances might leave us feeling overwhelmed but getting back to our hearts isn't difficult. Start with water, take a few deep breaths, make a nutritious treat run, and plan to go to bed early.

We put our health at risk when we sacrifice sleep to finish a project, believing this is the path to progress. The next morning, forcing yourself up as soon as possible, you gulp two cups of coffee and dive right in. But instead of progress on the project, hours are wasted with fits and starts, second-guessing, and frustration. The cost is a depleted immune system, less energy, foggier decisions.

Taking *physical* care of ourselves is the first need we sacrifice on a busy day, when a loved one is sick, or at the justification of doing what we want to do instead of what we need to do. We mistakenly think it's more urgent, important, noble, or strategic to invert the pyramid: put other people's needs first or finish a project instead of caring for ourselves.

But is that working for you? Is it bringing you the results you expected or hoped for? Is it solving your problems?

You might think you're prioritizing work, family, or something else, but how well can you do those jobs if you're working against yourself because you haven't planned for your physical well-being? A car needing an oil change will still run for a while. But if you put off maintenance for too long, you will pay the price in expensive repairs and lost time. You won't get as much milage out of an unmaintained car.

Sure, you can continue to run for a day, a week, or even a month of neglecting your physical needs. But you will eventually wear yourself out. When it comes to building a life you love—a truly beautiful life—if you do not care for your body in the process, you'll exhaust yourself trying.

Name the Big Rocks

A well-known time-management illustration features large rocks, small rocks, sand, water, and a jar.[17] The demonstration begins with a question: How might a person fit all this geology into a single jar?

The presenter first puts in the sand, then the small rocks. The jar is already almost full; there is clearly not enough space for the big rocks.

The presenter tries again, this time starting with the big rocks, then small rocks, then sand, then water. What didn't fit before now packs in the jar. It's a metaphor, of course, for life. The point is this: *the order of our priorities matters.* The principle holds whether you are organizing your day or planning your life. It only fits if we do things in the right order.

I love the nugget about the order of our priorities mattering. But, I have one frustration with this illustration. Will someone please tell me what the rocks are? The whole metaphor doesn't help you if you mislabel rocks as sand and sand as small pebbles.

The rocks-in-a-jar presentation leaves me asking what my rocks are. What goes in the jar first?

One of the advantages of HEART is the needs-based approach. So, you don't need to spend a lengthy time worrying about what goes first in your proverbial jar. You don't have to wonder anymore. The answer is the same for you, me, and everyone else. You start with your most basic needs: your physical ones.

We do not have to arbitrarily name the rocks or sand or water of our lives. Our human needs name them for us. Needs are something we were born with; we don't have to create them or find time. Our physical needs are the first rocks in the jar.

Write It Down, Make It Beautiful

1. What is your vision for building a healthy human body? What is the next most ideal version of your physical self?

2. What is one next step you could focus on in each of the following categories:
   - Sleep
   - Water
   - Nutrition
   - Movement

3. Make a list of things you could do daily to improve your physical well-being. Start small. Pick one easy thing from this list and commit to implementing it starting tomorrow.

Chapter 5

E–EMPOWER YOURSELF

"The soul never thinks without a picture."
ARISTOTLE

I saw a therapist for the first time in the winter of my ninth-grade year.

My mom was at her wit's end with me, and understandably so. I mean, who isn't at their wit's end with hormonal teenage daughters at some point? But I guess my adolescent angst was well past average on the drama scale.

Our school was about thirty minutes away from where we lived, and as I recall, the daily drive to school went smoothly. The pickup process must have been a bit more traumatic, at least for my mom, because one day she cut off my after-school string of woes, midsentence. "Whitney. Every day, you get into this car and melt. You unload, you cry, you complain. Everything is awful, terrible, and horrible. I can't handle it, Whitney. I don't know what to do with you."

I incited something, because she made an appointment with a family counselor and drove me to visit him one evening. This situation did not excite me. Therapists were for broken people, people who needed fixing. I wasn't sure what would happen in that session. It would probably involve him pointing out my mistakes and misgivings and giving me a list of things to change about myself. I wanted to "be better," but my defenses were on high alert. Fear and dread were standing in the wings, ready to jump in and fight at the first strike.

My mom must have sensed this, because while parking outside his office, she turned to me and said, "Whitney, there are two ways to look at this. You can choose to see this in a positive light or a negative light. If you choose to view it as a negative, you won't get anything out of it. But if you choose to see it as a positive, there's a chance you might learn something and grow."

Her words sunk in, and I opened the car door and headed into the office. A kind man about my height greeted me. He had thin hair, friendly eyes, and his office seemed cozy, more like a home than a doctor's office. He gestured to a sofa, and he sat in a chair opposite me. *Here it goes*, I thought with dread.

"So, tell me about yourself." His voice was soothing, and my threat alert level subsided. Elbows rested on the arms of the chair; he tented his fingers below his chin. There was a hint of a smile on his face, and he nodded occasionally. My words tumbled out as my subconscious realized I was safe.

I'm sure I only talked about whatever guy I had a crush on at the time in both sessions, and I only saw the therapist twice because he retired two months later. But in those two sessions, I realized my mom was right about a few things. First, my mindset, more than anything else, impacts how I see and experience my life. I can choose to see things in a positive light or a negative one. At the end of the day, my choices dictate what I get from any experience.

Second, I realized therapy isn't about what we say or what the therapist says to us; it's about what we learn. It matters because life gets a little easier when we become acquainted with what I refer to as our *inner world*. Even the inner world of a teenage girl, while probably neither rational nor remarkable (speaking from experience), plays a big role in her ability to maneuver her outer world (not to mention how miserable she makes the people who happen to reside in her outer world).

Understanding my inner world changed the way I understood myself and the way I experience my life, even to this day.

Years later, the therapist and his wife gave us a nice Spode bowl for our wedding. Every time I look at that bowl, I remember: one, I always have a choice; and two, knowing my inner world will always help me navigate my outer one.

Our Mindset and Our Inner World

I'm glad our culture is talking more about mindset and mental health. It's important. However, the way we talk about "having a positive mindset" makes it sound like you can slap a few positive affirmations on your bathroom mirror to transform your life into one identical to your favorite influencer's (or the version of it they post online).

Our inner worlds are gardens in need of tending. Just as our bodies demand daily care, our minds require consistent attention if we are to flourish. In a garden, the soil needs tilling, the roots need watering, and the plants need pruning to grow and flourish. The same is true for us and our minds.

One of the problems with traditional goal-setting is that it focuses too much on the external world and overlooks the internal one. It focuses on running the marathon or getting the raise or finding a spouse—forgetting the incredible depth of emotion, intellect, and spirit stirring under the surface when it comes to any of these objectives. That's what we are missing out on.

If you've ever tried to create something—a business, a family, a habit change—you know what I'm talking about. It's not about getting the job or cutting back on alcohol or completing the marathon. It's about how these things make us feel about ourselves in the process. It's about the person you become in the pursuit. It's as much about the process as it is about the final product.

When we overlook our inner world at the expense of our outer world, we miss the point.

Empower. It's the will to act and influence change. And to be truly empowered, we must understand the mechanics of our inner worlds.

When you wake up tomorrow and begin your morning routine, take notice. Your morning is not just coffee and breakfast and tying shoes and carpooling. Your morning is a delicate balance of emotions, preferences, and even the spiritual needs of the people involved. We've all had bad mornings.

The *E* Life Segment is here to remind us that, beyond our physical needs, we must meet critical intellectual, emotional, and spiritual needs to carry out the responsibilities we juggle each day. In the last chapter I used the example of a car going for months without an oil change. The analogy carries over here. Just because invisible emotions and thoughts happen outside the margins of our to-do list doesn't make them any less applicable to our everyday lives.

If you have an emotional meltdown, who will make lunches for your kids?

I say this tongue in cheek, but in all seriousness, I don't want us to miss this shift: when we pursue only external outcomes, we might achieve them, but miss out on the life meant for us. When we nurture our inner world, we *empower* ourselves to overcome mental battles and intercept obstacles to achieve anything we choose in the external world.

Then why are so many of us ignoring what's going on below the surface?

To help us become more acquainted with the inner workings of our minds, the *Empower Yourself* Life Segment has three checkpoints: mind, heart, and soul. If you want to be cute and stick with the *E* theme, you could think of it like this:

- Education: the data dots and how we connect them—also called intellect. In this checkpoint, we'll talk about empowerment through learning and intellectual growth.
- Emotions: feelings about yourself, your circumstances, and the people and world around you. In this checkpoint, we'll discuss empowerment through feeling and heart.
- Edification: the spirit or the soul. This is our higher self, the part of us more in touch with our greater purpose (or sometimes not).

Confused? That's okay. Many of us avoid our inner worlds—because they are complicated and fragile, and didn't come with IKEA instructions. But that's part of why we need to learn how to navigate them. The ability to comprehend our thoughts and express our feelings is a superpower. The outer world can be in total chaos around us, but when our inner worlds are at peace, *we* are at peace.

Our inner worlds might look scary and feel uncomfortable, as we confront our anxieties, acknowledge our wounds, and take stock of our thought patterns. Visiting these depths not only seems like a bother and nuisance but we know the real reason we don't go there. We might be forced to face difficult realities, embrace uncertainty, and disrupt our fragile state.

It's much easier to dismiss our doubts, fears, and insecurities than risk the awkwardness of a confrontation. We tell ourselves things like:

- I must push forward.
- Big girls don't cry.
- It's pointless to dwell on it.
- Don't go there.

Or, the heroic one: *I'm fine.* (According to a friend, this stands for Feeling Insecure, Neurotic, and Emotional, which sounds about right.)

But we're not fine. We're anxious, hurt, frustrated, angry, lonely, confused, and in dire need of a break. Thank goodness the real world offers a bevy of distractions! With so much to do and achieve in the outside world, we can safely avoid dealing with our inner chaos. But in reality, it is our job to call out the internal commotion, not to cave to it.

As soon as we name our emotions, they lose their power over us. Instead of telling ourselves what we think we want to hear, what if we told ourselves the gentle truth? What if, instead of focusing on our accomplishments, we admitted that we truly want to be seen and loved by the people we care about the most? It's ludicrous to think our emotions don't matter or that they will resolve on their own. We convince ourselves all we need to keep us going is food, water, and money in the bank. But the truth is we need more.

Our brains and bodies don't know this. We tell them by acknowledging and naming them. Remember that time you tried to hold back tears because you didn't want to seem weak? What if you named it? "I'm feeling overwhelmed. Please excuse me." And then excused yourself to the bathroom, and looked in the mirror and complimented yourself? Reminded your inner you that you love her and are proud of her?

Ignoring our inner world has serious repercussions. Never before has this been more apparent than in the period of time we're living in. Our outer world is in chaos. We are living through a global health crisis, unprecedented political tension, a gut-wrenching rise in gun violence, senseless murders, genocides—which doesn't even touch on our personal lives. Change and transition are causing divisions among family and friends, as well as unprecedented financial instability.

Sit with that a minute. It's impossible not to feel sad.

We live in a broken world, which is all the more reason to have a strong handle on our inner world. My guess is: this is hard for you. That's normal. It's hard for me too. But acknowledging and naming your feelings is the place to start. And there is so much freedom on the other side.

When times are difficult, finding that good stillness in my inner world has become a matter of survival. So rather than write this section off, let's pause for a minute and scan the following questions. Check in with your inner self. How are you doing—really?

Name what you are feeling right now:

- How is your spirit? Do you feel safe and nourished or are you just getting by?
- When was the last time your mind was stimulated in a meaningful way?
- How often do you feel anxious or stressed?
- Is it hard to make decisions? What's happening in your mind when you try?
- Are you having trouble falling or staying asleep?
- Do you find yourself unmotivated to wake up in the morning?
- Do you commonly experience feelings of helplessness or hopelessness?
- Are you having obsessive or recurring thoughts?
- Is it difficult to concentrate on the task at hand?
- Do you feel isolated?

- Who are the people who make you feel understood? How often do you connect with these people?

We get sidetracked when we're not in the right mental state. When we are not fully present in our tasks or relationships, we become irritable and anxious. We can't sleep. We neglect our people and cut ourselves off from those who might help us. We feel isolated. When we can't focus on what's in front of us, we can't bring our best to the project at hand.

Insecurities and phobias drive us to make judgments based on irrationality rather than logic, love, or compassion. This behavior is easier to recognize in others than in ourselves. Every month, I get a call from a dear friend who wants to catch up. She rattles off the frustrations of her life: she's worried about her son, frustrated with her sister, and unsure whether or not to sign up her daughter for soccer. She is always worked up and talking a mile a minute. When I ask her what's wrong, she always tells me she's exhausted and doesn't know "where to start!"

She's a dear friend, and I think she calls me because she knows I've been there. Her frustrations are always genuine, honest, and gracious. Her situation is stressful, and even though she's not complaining, I know their family is tight on money this year. Listening to her, I hear she has a full plate. She isn't practicing self-care or soul-care. I can't tell if she's looking for answers or accepting her current circumstances with mixed feelings.

I've known her for a long time. When it comes to dealing with the stresses of family life, she's more than competent. But her *inner world* isn't empowering her to be her best self. If she doesn't find a way to nurture and nourish her inner world, things might get more difficult.

The good news is she has a variety of options for empowering herself.

The Checkpoints: Mind, Heart, Soul

When it comes to personal awareness and self-evaluation, I use three words to keep me grounded: mind, heart, and soul. These three checkpoints provide a tool to evaluate my balance and point me to next steps.

Mind

For the sake of this discussion, consider your mind as the hub of your thinking. In this hub, we store memories, create, organize, and solve issues. Not bad for such a small object! (Pat your brain on the back and thank it immediately, okay?)

We expect a lot of our minds!

But here's my next question: What do our minds need from us?

Aside from our brain's physical needs, we can support our brain in other ways. Reading, writing, listening to podcasts, taking courses, and journaling can all help prepare our minds to complete their daily tasks.

I want to offer a simple technique I use to get in touch with my innermost thoughts. I start by sitting up, getting comfortable, and listening to my body. My physical needs must be met before I can focus, so I run to the bathroom, or wash my face—whatever it takes to get comfortable. Nice smells help too. (Some people call this a bubble bath.) When I'm finished pampering myself, I pull out a journal and pen.

What have I been consuming? Billboards? TV Commercials? Pinterest? Instagram? Books? A screen? Nature? Art? What have I been learning? Discussing? What has my digital footprint looked like this week? How do I feel about these things? Name the feelings.

What have I been creating? Words and paragraphs? Paint on canvas? Thread to needle? How was my day?

I leave the "how was my day?" question until the end, because if I started there, I'd never get to the other two topics, which are easier to answer and more important. What I've been consuming causes me to face reality. Everything I do is pretty much documented in this day and age. What time I woke up, when my heart rate went up, how many steps I got in, how much screen time I used, and what I looked at in those moments. Heck, Alexa may even be listening to me yell at my kids—who knows? Since the answers to this question are so easy to determine, it quickly gives me a deeply honest perspective on my life. When I don't like the answers to my questions, I change my behavior: less screen time, more patience, no doom-scrolling, more walks.

The answers to the second group of questions tell me what I've been working on and how

I'm giving back. There's nothing more beautiful: the sharing of your soul, so bravely, with our beloved, broken world.

The answers to the third question help me reduce speed. Why reflect on a day I've barely finished? Reflection brings a new perspective, giving us insight and understanding into our actions. And I don't need to convince you we could all use a slow-down.

Listening to how I answer these questions gives me insight about where I could shift my focus. I'm less concerned about if I *should* shift my focus. I'm a grown adult. I know what I should do. The problem is I don't always do it. This is because I have made a choice, within my control, not to prioritize it. I can choose, going forward, to do it or not to do it. The least I can do is not beat myself up about my choices and not overcommit my future self.

The world will shame us enough, friends, if we let it. I will not let my own heart, soul, and mind jump on that bandwagon. There's a better way to equip myself.

Heart

I know, I know. It's what this whole book is about.

Those three questions will resuscitate many feelings. When you think about the word *heart*, think about your emotional well-being. Our hearts dictate:

- Our self-esteem: how we feel about ourselves on any given day.
- Our perspective: how we feel about life's ups and downs.
- Our empathy: how we feel about people.
- Our resilience: how we feel when we're mistreated, betrayed, or abused. (Do you feel empowered to make a choice and set a boundary, for example, or do you feel trapped?)
- Our confidence: how we feel about our ability to create change in our circumstances.
- Our self-compassion: how we talk to ourselves. (Is your inner dialogue critical or compassionate?)

Have you ever had your emotions take you by surprise at an inopportune time? One moment you're fine, and the next, it's waterworks central with emotions pouring out for everyone to see.

Everything you've been avoiding, everything you've been stuffing deep, confronts you. This is one of the pitfalls of ignoring our emotional health.

Apathy always results in a loss of motivation. Emotions are fuel for our actions. When we overlook our emotional world (for fear of what it contains), we suppress the engine that drives many daily decisions. No wonder we procrastinate, or feel tired and disconnected! Numbness simply cannot produce the same quality of life that healthy emotion provides.

Speaking of which, two major symptoms of ignoring the emotions of our heart are meltdown and burnout. Maybe these feelings sound familiar to you. I know they do to me. When we don't check in with our hearts, we lose sight of what we need, we allow ourselves to revert to old habits and patterns, and we eventually fall apart.

To check in with our hearts, here are a few questions we can ask ourselves:

- How am I feeling?
- Where in my body am I experiencing these feelings?
- Am I hurt? Grieving? Angry? Scared?
- Am I happy or grateful?
- Is there something from my past holding me back today?
- How do I feel about the future?

Checking in with my emotional heart gives me insight into the feelings that influence my outlook, beliefs, and decisions. Awareness won't eliminate these emotions, but it will empower us to understand our feelings and support a healthy mind.

Soul

Of these three elements, the soul is perhaps the most difficult to define. But we talk about it all the time. We find soul mates, do soul-searching, and have soul sisters. People have been known to bare their souls, sell their souls, and lose their souls. There are gentle souls, old souls, satisfied and hungry souls. For as little as we understand it, culturally it seems we all agree it's an important part of who we are.

When we discuss the soul here, I'm talking about the higher self, the part of us that feels connected to something bigger than we are. This is your intuition, the gut instinct that just knows, and your sense of purpose in the world.

Our souls are an influential part of who we are. You could think of your soul as a majority shareholder, a board member with a controlling interest in our lives. Our souls have a lot of sway in how we feel, think, and live. But they're quiet, and easily forgotten. And many of us are ignoring our souls.

Our souls help us:

- feel connected to our community,
- feel a sense of purpose and order in life (even when it doesn't make sense),
- know in a deep way we are loved,
- experience a sense of awe,
- trust that we are supported, and
- surrender to difficult circumstances, trusting there is a bigger meaning.

We all have a soul, and many of our souls are desperate for refreshment. So many souls wander this planet, feel lonely or disconnected, and wonder why they're here or if any of this matters. A well-kept soul is a deep well from which we can draw strength when we face challenges.

We need to regularly check in with our souls. I used to disregard this soul-care stuff as new-age propaganda, but maturity has helped me understand the value of the soul. We must cling to an inner anchor, or we will perish in the outer storm. In the next section, we will brainstorm ways we can nourish our souls, but for now, here are some questions to ask yourself.

- Do I feel connected to myself?
- Do I feel connected to others?
- Do I feel connected to nature and the physical world?
- Do I feel connected to God?
- Have I prayed or meditated today?

It is in our souls that we feel connection and purpose. We can discount the spiritual, the unseen, but I remind myself humans have only recently begun to overlook the spiritual part of our lives. In the outside world, things may not be going as planned, but in my inner world I feel a deep sense that I am safe and everything will be okay. With regular soul-tending, we will feel anchored in the midst of chaos.

Doing these check-ins might not fix anything right away. In fact, if you're not used to turning to your inner world, at first you might feel as though paying attention to your thoughts, emotions, or soul makes you feel more anxious, rather than less. It might make things—for a time—more chaotic than they were before. Remember, discomfort means we're growing. (I know, I hate it too.)

Don't write off these checkpoints. We experience transformation when we routinely tend our physical, emotional, intellectual, and spiritual needs. We make better decisions. We find conviction to say no to things not meant for us. We break the cycle of overcommitment. We gain clarity about the future while we focus on the road ahead. We navigate muddled and messy days without losing hope or our sense of self.

This is the power of the inner world. This is the gift of knowing what is happening under the surface.

Nurturing Your Inner World

To live a more beautiful life, we must be honored to invest in our emotions, thoughts, and spirit. This is key to HEART. We can host the parties, achieve the goals, make the friends, but the beauty of our inner world will stay locked away. Stuck in the rat race of accomplishing and doing and surviving, finding the path to these hidden worlds can feel impossible.

What I'm about to tell you isn't a big secret. We know these things; we just don't do them. As you explore the list below, consider how you could incorporate these practices into your daily life.

Just focus on one, to start. Schedule overhaul not required here. We're not looking for radical transformation, that's too big picture. Shoot for two or three degrees of change.

Reflecting on your answers to the questions above, which of the tools below will deepen your understanding of your inner world?

Discovering Your Inner World

Journeying into our inner world is a rewarding experience, even if it is a harrowing road. The paradigm shifts and beliefs below eased my travels.

Therapy is for everyone. Meeting with a licensed therapist can help. I know this from personal experience and countless testimonies of women around me who have confronted and overcome some of their deepest wounds in therapy. Therapy can bring resolution, peace, and healing to emotional wounds. It can empower you to move forward with your life.

Don't wait until it's an emergency. While that sofa in the office may seem threatening at first, you'll soon learn to trust it. If you've tried therapy before and had a bad experience, I encourage you to try again. If you don't like the therapist, find a new one. Don't give up on your inner work. In therapy, you can process thoughts and feelings before sharing with others. The benefit of a therapist is their objectivity. A therapist is a safe place to vent, grieve, brainstorm, and confide.

Go somewhere green. Just as nature regulates our bodies, the good ol' outdoors influences our thoughts, emotions, and spirit. Employ your senses: feel the sunshine on your skin, drink in the fresh air, and shake out your stiff limbs. Note the scents and sounds, taking a minute to appreciate the moment. If you're in a big city, find a park or a green space.

Pray or meditate. I don't know about you, but I thought they had gone off the deep end when someone first suggested meditation to me. I thought I knew what meditation was, but I didn't understand the benefits to the human body. So, I wrote it off. Big mistake. This practice involves quieting our thoughts, bodies, and breathing. Meditation taught me how to let things go and allow thoughts to pass without judgment or unhealthy emotion. On the floor or in a chair, focused on our breath, we give our bodies a reset. Even if you're in your office, trying to work but up to your ears in ankle biters, that minute of breathing is a gift to your body. Skeptics, you don't have to go to yoga; there are lots of meditation podcasts. And I say you get triple the impact if you couple it with prayer. When I pray, before I panic, I may still panic, but my mind, emotions, and spirit are better prepared for battle. Meditation over medication.

Give prayer a try, even if you don't consider yourself a spiritual person. I think God listens to everybody, even if we're not talking to Him. Prayer is nothing but a reverent pause and an admission that we know we are not in control.

Plugging into a spiritual community might also serve you well. It is reassuring to feel and know we are part of something bigger and not alone in the journey.

Reach out to a friend. Vulnerability is risky, but incredibly healing. You need trustworthy friends, ones who will keep your confidence and treat you with respect and compassion. When considering who to confide in, ask yourself: *Are they honest? Do they speak well of those not present? Do they talk about people, or things, or ideas? How do they make you feel? Do they want the best for you? Do they boss you around, or help you figure it out? Do they have good judgment?*

Trusted friends can relieve stress, provide clarity, offer stability, and give you strength. Even if they don't understand, having them listen can allow you to feel heard, worthy, and more confident. Our external factors may remain the same, but our ability to handle the situation improves.

Read self-help books. You are not alone. So much of our human experience is familiar to others. Reading self-help books or memoirs of those with similar experiences allows you to benefit from the wisdom of people who've been in your shoes.

Take a personality assessment. Learning my Myers-Briggs Type and Enneagram number has been life-changing. Personality assessments give us an objective view of our thinking, motivators, and habits. Personality typing systems make for great dinner party conversation, opening new lines of communication and connection. I enjoy diving into Enneagram number discussions. When someone asks my number, they give me the big smiling nod, along with a considerable "Ahh." This is universal language for "now I get you." If you don't know what these are, don't sweat. A plethora of personality assessments can be found online. They might give you that aha moment you need to observe yourself with more compassion.

Focus on the positive. When we feel irritated, annoyed, or stressed because of our circumstances, these negative emotions leech into our lives. We start to doubt the possibility of a positive outcome. We make a mistake when we replay our mistakes. But we have a choice: descend into a cycle of despair or take ownership of our outcomes. Do we overlook the bad, or honestly acknowledge it, before moving on to seeing the good and spotting the possibilities? Do we allow the big picture to scare us, or do we dive into the details that will build better experiences? Am I choosing to learn and grow? The upward spiral begins when we focus on positive takeaways and learn from present circumstances. This mental shift is the power of a positive mindset.

These are by no means all the ways to nurture your inner world. Nor are these all the questions you could ask yourself about your inner world—but they are a start.

I can't tell you whether ten minutes or an hour a day will change everything for you, but I promise small steps add up to big results. Like astronauts on a rocket ship, with their sights set on the moon. Thirty minutes of reading won't change my life, but it will change my afternoon. That's the two-degree shift we are looking for. And when you are trying to reach the moon, two degrees is dramatic. It's the difference between landing on the moon and ending up in a different galaxy.

Where are you ending up?

No Need to Fall Apart

I came face-to-face with why our inner worlds are so essential at a moment when I was doing very well in my outer world but hadn't been consistently tending to my inner world.

I was sitting on the side of a cliff at an entrepreneurial retreat, with a bunch of strangers. The retreat sounded like a good idea when my friend suggested it. I had second thoughts, though, at several points.

There was at least one bestselling author in my small group, a few Grammys floating around, and maybe a reality TV star, though I wouldn't recognize them. One thing was painfully obvious: I was a mistake. I did not belong here with these people. No siree. They had invited the wrong girl.

If I had to name the feeling, it would have been, "I do not deserve this." Humility? Modesty? No, because I could name more than a handful of times when I had been neither humble nor modest about my accomplishments. Was it shame? How did someone who had filed for business bankruptcy, never written a book, and had few scant highlights get invited? What could I possibly contribute?

This is the thing with our inner worlds. No matter what happens outside, our inner worlds have their own ideas. If we listen to the critical Neocortex Crew, we'll never win. And the lizards are horrible communicators. But this whole thing is like an action movie where the bad guy ends up being the good guy in a plot twist at the end.

I've always been painfully aware of my lack of executive function. My school book bag was disorganized. I drew gumball machines on my math papers in high school. I didn't get a college scholarship. I was the member in bad standing in both my sorority *and* the junior league. At the stationery store, a customer ridiculed me because I didn't know how to count back change. A former employee, years my senior, once proclaimed I was "not fit for leadership" as she closed the door to my office.

Without a doubt, friends. Not the right person for this cliffside entrepreneurial retreat.

Au contraire, mon frère.

Here's the thing about good humans: they all see you as one of them. You are not an imposter who got a few lucky breaks. You are not what others label you as: athlete, basket case, princess, or criminal. You are beautifully, wonderfully, perfectly, and only *you*. Deserving of every good thing heading your way. Say thank you for it.

Still on the side of those cliffs, no matter how much I tried to talk myself out of it, I melted, crying until I couldn't talk. Shoulders shaking, lips quivering, unable to speak, and struggling to reconcile why such a fantastic group of people had invited me on their retreat.

Basket case, party of one.

Friends, what I am about to tell you changed my life.

Trust the process.

In my small group was the CEO of an experiential therapy center called Onsite. At the time, I had no idea what the heck experiential therapy was. Still, it had the word *therapy* in it, so

I looked at Miles in the middle of my meltdown and said, "I guess I'll be enrolling for the next session," and he looked back at me and said, "We'd love to help you."

It wasn't long after this fiasco that I pulled up the Onsite web page and registered. It was a huge commitment; this wasn't one therapy session or even a weekly trip to a sofa in an office. This was a week-long intensive, with group activities, morning meditations and educational classes, and vulnerable group sessions. But that's what basket cases need, right? I plowed forward.

I drove myself to a small town outside Nashville, parked my car, and proceeded to the registration table. After putting my gear in my cabin, I made my way to the orientation session, where I learned the ground rules for the week:

1) You can't say your last name.
2) You can't talk about what you do.
3) No phones.

Upon this proclamation, the facilitators produced a set of labels, pre-printed with our first names. One by one they collected our phones until the label sheet was empty. Each labeled phone went into a box. For a week. Talk about forcing you to focus on your *inner* world.

I had no idea what I was getting into.

It was the best thing I've ever done.

I went to bed without a phone. To pass the time, I read the first few chapters of a mystery. At some point, I fell asleep. Without a phone. It was the first time in weeks, if not years.

From that point on, the retreat was a blur. There wasn't much talking, surprisingly. No kumbaya. There were writing exercises: letters to yourself in the future, the past, family-of-origin diagramming kind of stuff. We learned about the amygdala and lizard brain and taking ownership so you don't become a victim.

At the end of the week, when we sat in the orientation room for the final time, I looked around the circle and knew fifty-two other people's first names—names I had not known until six days earlier. In almost all those cases, I knew stories. I'd witnessed brokenness, vulnerability, fear, shame, and desperation. I had no idea who these people were, what they did for a living, what they were proud of, or what life circumstances had brought them to this point. But it was the safest place I'd ever stood, because I had held their pain when they'd shared it. And they had held mine.

We all just want our pain to be seen, our words to be heard, and our hearts to be loved. What a lesson in the inner world. At Onsite, they called it a "two-degree shift," because that's the difference between hitting the moon and missing.

After that, I saw myself in a new light. I felt more compassion for my "inner child" (a concept I had once mocked). I understood the way I operated. I learned to forgive myself and those who might have wronged me.

E for Essential

At the end of the day, it's not that we just want a more beautiful life. We want to be seen, heard, known, and loved. This feeds into our desire for connection, confidence, and an even deeper need for purpose and peace. It may feel like a detour to shift your focus from ambitions to inner world, but it's not. I promise.

You might be worried your life is too messy or unfixable. You may think change takes too long, that it's easier to skip this part and go for the outer world achievements. I know from personal experience that it won't work.

Our bodies support us as we move through the day. But our minds, hearts, and souls regulate our motivations, our experiences, our narratives, and how we see ourselves. Ignore that, and you ignore everything.

If we are to be our best selves, do our best work, and love our people well, if we are to live the life we were created for, we must not neglect our inner world.

Small things began to change. I spent less time worrying about my appearance, while at the same time taking better care of myself physically. If I heard the tiny voice of shame, I noticed and regrouped. New, kinder programming replaced old beliefs. I took a step back and reevaluated when I felt pressured to accomplish something. I asked myself where that desperate feeling was coming from. When I neglected my emotions, I fell apart, but when I confronted and owned my story, wounds, wins, and all, I was empowered to take ownership of my life.

Working on our inner worlds does not require us to register for a week-long therapy camp. You can make daily, weekly, and monthly progress without lifting a finger. This is a heart choice—you just need to convince your head to come along. (The exercises at the end of this chapter will help too.)

Don't overlook your inner world. Your outer world ambitions may be achievable, but what's the point if you still doubt yourself? Confidence comes before achievement. When you care for, understand, and nurture a strong inner world, it doesn't matter what else you do or don't accomplish. You empower yourself to create the life you were designed for.

And it's pretty beautiful.

Write It Down, Make It Beautiful

1. What do a healthy mind and healthy emotions look like for you?
2. What is your ideal vision for the spiritual part of your life?

3. What could you do to focus on improving your intellect?
4. How can you focus on getting in touch with your emotions and feelings?
5. What practices help you to be present, focused, and compassionate to yourself and others?
6. How can you familiarize yourself and get comfortable with a more focused spiritual practice?
7. What are some actions you can take? What are some things you'd like to read?
8. What would you like to journal about?
9. What new spiritual practices might you like to incorporate? If you're not ready to dive in, go someplace familiar, but remember, goodness happens on the other side of your comfort zone.

Chapter 6

A–ALL YOUR PEOPLE

"Plans provide a framework for our day, but people fill our day with heart."

MS. JILL WHITE, MY FIFTH GRADE TEACHER

A dear friend invited me to a baby shower recently. It may seem trivial, but in the context of my life at the time, it was monumental.

For starters, this was in the spring of 2021. We had just spent the past year quarantined in our homes, wary of any outside interaction. When we did leave, it was with masks on our faces and trepidation in our hearts. No one wanted to get sick.

Considering the state of the world in 2020 and 2021, I hadn't traveled much. It had been at least eighteen months since I'd seen my friends in Nashville, Tennessee—a good day's drive from where I live in Oklahoma. So, when my friend Betsy invited me to her baby shower that spring, it wasn't just a baby shower.

It was an opportunity to reconnect with people who are important to me.

I said yes immediately. I made the commute. And then I cried the whole way home. I cried because it had felt so good to connect with friends. I cried because, after a terrifying year, I felt supported and surrounded by people who loved me and reminded me who I was.

Not seeing our friends was the least of our concerns during the days of COVID lockdown. Or so I told myself. We had political unrest, community conflicts, a global health crisis, canceled schools, loss of jobs, lonely loved ones, and all of this compounded by the fear of serious illness. Survival mode was the order of the season as we navigated homeschool, childcare, careers, and a very real toilet paper shortage.

If you're like me, you relegated the lack of friend connections to the bottom of your concerns list. Sure, you missed seeing your friends, but with so many other concerns, it wasn't pressing. When I realized I was missing that sense of connection, I made quick efforts to bring my relationships back into balance.

Do you ever feel as though your relationships are out of balance? Maybe you push them aside in an extra busy season of work, to-dos, responsibilities, and obligations? Or do you feel like well-meaning relationships are smothering you at times, and are lacking *real* connection?

Do any of these feel familiar?

- Maybe you've been burned, scarred, or hurt by people in the past.
- Maybe you feel uncertain, like you don't know how to make friends.
- Maybe you feel insecure, worrying people won't like you once they get to know you.
- Maybe you worry you're not giving enough to your relationships.
- Maybe you worry you are focusing on too many relationships simultaneously, causing all your relationships to suffer.
- Maybe your phone is blowing up all day, every day, and you love all the excitement and energy from friends, but feel like you are neglecting family.

The *All Your People* Life Segment reminds us of the importance of our relationships and helps us cultivate and balance our relationships so we can be successful in the other Life Segments, as well.

You deserve meaningful, fulfilling, life-giving, happy relationships. You deserve a romantic relationship that feels supportive and contented (if you want). You deserve to have a rich and rewarding relationship with your children. You deserve to have friends you can call when you're having a bad day or are in a crisis. You deserve to be heard. In this chapter, I'll share some tools to strengthen this area of your life if it doesn't feel like it's quite there (and tools for maintenance if my description feels right on track).

Why Relationships?

The *A* in HEART is for *All Your People* because no matter how inconvenient, complex, or demanding relationships feel, they matter.

We are relational beings.

Spiritually, relational needs run deep. We are designed for connection. In addition to needing relationships for our emotional health, relationships kept us alive. Back in the caveman days, when the lizard brain worked much harder, groups and tribes meant safety and survival.

But the need for relationships doesn't stop there. The importance of relationships is not about being in general relationship with others. It's about creating the kinds of relationships where *love* flows. When we create mutually beneficial relationships, we benefit others, and we are filled with light and love.

And yet somehow relationships have a way of either falling to the bottom of the priority list or taking up so much space in our minds that we can't seem to get much else done. The result? We don't have many meaningful relationships.

Relationships are a huge factor in what makes everyday life worth living. We enjoy relationships. Relationships motivate us. They can transform our work and duties, making the mundane meaningful. Relationships can make painful experiences purposeful, and they can bring us joy and solace in tough times. Even our most difficult relationships shape us into the people we are. Take a minute and think about some difficult relationships and what you have learned by setting boundaries and giving yourself space.

Relationships matter the same way self-care (H) and soul-care (E) matter. Without all of our people, we cannot function at our highest and best. If we downgrade relationships on our priority list, or elevate them above our own needs, it's not just bad for our people; it's bad for *us*.

Relationships aren't easy. You know this because you've had a friend, a sibling, a parent, a child, or a spouse. Relationships are challenging and changing as we move through seasons of life. We go from single to married and our needs change. When we have kids, our relational needs change; we need different kinds of support from our partner and friends. When our kids go to college, our relational needs will change again.

Relationships have a knack for triggering emotional responses that completely derail us (and send us right back to Life Segment E). If you've ever yelled at your kids when you were having a bad day, rolled your eyes at a passing comment from a parent, had a tense and awkward conversation with a friend, or stormed out of the house when your partner did "that thing" again, you know what I'm talking about.

So how do we manage this complicated balance of relationships? How do we build meaningful connections with the people around us? How do we create that positive flow of love I mentioned before? How can relationships fuel us while still requiring energy for growth?

Without the answer to this question, we risk going through life without one of the fundamental basic needs: connection to others.

When you're connected to others, you're capable of more. You've heard it said, "Two are better than one." That's both spiritually and practically true. How much can you accomplish when you have someone you love helping you, standing by you, holding your hand? Life is more fun when we do it together. If the pandemic lockdown taught us anything, it taught us this: the mundane occurrences of daily life aren't as meaningful when we're disconnected from those we long to share it with.

Souls matter. Starting with yours. The nourishment of the human soul comes through relationships because we are *relational beings*. So, if you feel lonely, isolated, unseen, or like you haven't gotten the hang of being in relationship—if you find yourself frustrated with unsatisfactory relationships with your spouse, your neighbors, your family members, or your friends—let's learn to nurture and cherish those connections by going deeper. But first, let's discuss this positioning of the *All Your People* Life Segment.

The Mistakes We Make

When it comes to relationships, people tend to make a couple of mistakes.

The first mistake so many of us make is thinking that relationships aren't important—that life is all about you and your agenda. You might know people like this. I know I do. It's not that I don't value my relationships. I just sometimes act like they aren't important. I get caught up in life, my schedule, and duties and forget to intentionally love on my people.

We *need* relationships—we need them to be happy and thrive as human beings. The largest longitudinal study that's ever been done in its field is called The Harvard Study (sometimes referred to as the Harvard happiness study). The researchers found, after tracking a group of men from college through late years, that the people who reported the most happiness were the ones with the best relationships.[1]

So deprioritizing our relationships isn't the answer.

But the second mistake people make when it comes to relationships can be just as disrupting to our lives. If the data and my personal experience ring true, you might relate more to this second mistake than to the first. That is, we let our relationships come before our own physical, mental, emotional, and spiritual needs. The second mistake is an inverse of the first.

Do you ever find yourself stressed and worried about the neighbor who needs you to pick up his packages, the new mom who needs a lasagna, the fundraiser you agreed to chair, the text message you forgot to return, the friend you haven't heard from in several months, the cousin going through a health scare, a child struggling in school, another child struggling emotionally, your husband's birthday tomorrow . . . should I go on? Does this sound too familiar?

If you're like most women I know, you *know* that relationships matter. You care about your people. You want them to succeed. And so you persistently pour into everyone you meet.

But it's possible to invest too much in too many people. And when you do this, everybody suffers.

Obviously, altogether disregarding relationships is one issue. But overinvesting in *too many* relationships is equally damaging and dangerous. Take a minute to think about what your tendency is with relationships.

Do you overinvest?

Underinvest?

Or maybe you find yourself, ever so confusingly, fluctuating between the two.

Either way, the *All Your People* Life Segment is meant to help us bring our relationships back into balance.

I know I can cut corners here, prioritizing others at the expense of myself, but I won't be able to love others to the best of my ability—because I won't be at my best. Then again, if I hyper-focus on my goals and objectives, without investing HEART into my people, I'm setting myself up for destructive relationships.

The Bible says, "Love your neighbor as yourself" (Matthew 19:19 ESV). To make it even more explicit: love your neighbor as you *love* yourself. First, love yourself. Then you can love others the way God wants us to.

But the question remains: How do we strike that oh-so-difficult balance?

The Steps to Healthy Relationships

As a way to help you strike a balance between overinvesting and underinvesting in relationships that matter to you, we will walk through a process I've been using for nearly ten years. These steps might seem a bit formulaic at first, but I use this to do a basic check-in and decide how much I can invest in relationships (and which ones) over the course of a week or a month.

The process is four simple steps:

Step 1: Know who my people are.

Step 2: Evaluate my relationships.

Step 3: Ask, *What can I realistically give?*

Step 4: Give according to my capacity.

Know Who My People Are

You were not meant for everyone. That's a hard pill for a people-pleaser to swallow, but it's true. Sometimes you'll show love to someone who is not your person—the man on the corner asking for change, the child at church who needs help, the woman standing in front of you in the grocery store. In some ways, *all* people are "your" people, in that we are called to love everybody.

But what I mean by "your" people is that if you try to love all people, all the time, without ever focusing on yourself, you're on the fast track to burnout. And nobody does a very good job of loving anybody when they're burnt-out (*I say from experience*).

It is helpful to identify the people I am called to regularly and intentionally pour love into. When there is overflow to give, who should be the first in line to get this overflow?

I like to use visuals, and mental models can reinforce our understanding, so I built a graphic using concentric circles. I'll walk you through the exercise below.

Make a list. On a piece of paper, list your people. All of them: family, friends, coworkers, community members, neighbors, and nice guys.

Check your text messages, think about who you've emailed or called. And don't forget online connections.

Look at your list. Chances are, it's *long*. Do you feel overwhelmed seeing all the names together? The reason for prioritizing is clear, right? Imagine if you had to remember every single birthday, special occasion, or need of every person on that list. What if you had to do regular check-ins with all of them? What a nightmare! And yet many of us have been unconsciously trying to do this.

Draw your concentric circles—meaning four circles, one inside the other.

It should look like this:

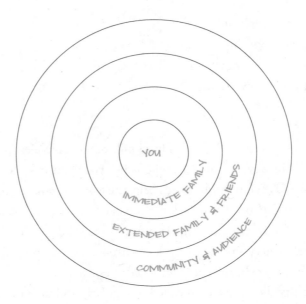

Circle 1: Who am I responsible for?

Inside your smallest circle, list the people you are responsible for. This could be your kids, aging parents, a partner, or a longtime friend. These are our most important relationships, the ones we want to invest in, even when they require our maximum time and attention.

My friend Bob likes to say that about eight people will fit around your deathbed. It's a morbid image but also a helpful one—consider the eight people you'd want by your side as you take your final breath.

Keep it to ten or less.

Circle 2: Which relationships bring me life and energy?

In your second circle, directly outside the first one, list the relationships that add value to your life—without your having to work hard to maintain them. This second tier includes relationships that have give-and-take, of course, but include friends you can pick up where you left off with.

This circle contains extended family and close friends. These are people you text, call, and meet up with, especially when you need a relational boost.

Like your first list, this can't be an unlimited number of people. We are limited beings. Again, try to keep this list from five to ten.

Circle 3: Who can I serve?

In circle 3, write the names of some communities (not necessarily individuals) where you could serve. Think about what your gifts are and how you could use those gifts to serve. Maybe you serve in the nursery at church, or you like to volunteer at your local food bank, or your gifts are best used by meeting with young creatives or professionals in transition to help them figure out what's next.

Don't just think about who needs you. Who do you need? What contributions give you the most joy? Is this your team at work? A local church? A creative meeting you attend once a month? Your writing group or book club?

Circle 4: Who is left?

Identify relationships on the peripheries of your life. This could include acquaintances who you know from work, a friend of a friend who often reaches out, or a neighbor who waves when you walk by their house. Here's a list that can easily become lengthy, and that's okay. As you write these names, how do you feel? Grateful? Annoyed? Warm and fuzzy? Pay attention to how you feel.

Do you feel drained when you think about interacting with certain people? Guilty? It's important to realize that some of these relationships might need a demotion on your priority list.

Who are your five? This exercise is meant to help us focus our energy and attention on the relationships that truly deserve it. Nobody can be everybody's best friend. Nobody can meet everybody's needs. And our relationships improve—become richer and more fulfilling—when we know which ones to prioritize.

Next, looking at your concentric circles, jot down *five relationships* you plan to keep in your inner circle. Of course, if you have five children and a spouse, adjust this exercise to make it work for you. Immediate family is most likely on your inner-circle list. But if you're like me and you have three children and a spouse, you'll see how quickly your list of five writes itself.

So this is why we've been fighting relationship tension! We've been working with a list of thirty when most of us can only handle five.

The first time I did this exercise, a light bulb came on. By trying to keep everyone else happy, I was taxing myself, and my favorite five were paying the price.

Since prioritizing my favorite five relationships, I have extra energy for needs outside of my five. This is possible because I've placed the needs of those closest to me right next to my own. I'm less likely to have a chaotic day putting out fires. I'm more likely to be rested and settled in my own skin. I can respond to unexpected requests with grace and compassion.

People before projects multiplies productivity.

All because of my favorite five.

You don't have to have a favorite five. You can have a super six or a sensational seven or an amazing eight. You just can't have a wonderful one-fifty.

Figure out your capacity. A great way to do this is to note the number of meaningful conversations you have every day before you hit a wall. When you hit your daily wall (we all have one), count the number of meaningful conversations you had before the wall. That's your capacity. Know it. Trust it. Lean into what you were designed to be.

This exercise infuses our relationships with intention and purpose. We can filter experiences and opportunities. If you have extra capacity one week, perhaps you'll offer to bring a meal to the woman from church who recently had a baby. Or you'll make a special stop at the neighbor's house to drop off cookies. When you're already at max capacity and an acquaintance from work asks you to dinner, you have the clarity to say, "That won't work for me right now."

This past weekend, my daughter asked, "What can we play, Mom?" Basically, she was asking me to stop working. It was a Sunday night, and having already worked all weekend, I had failed to prioritize those inner-circle relationships. This is the clarity that our concentric circles bring. They help us make choices about what matters.

One final word on ending relationships. This exercise may reveal a relationship that needs to be demoted, deprioritized, or given boundaries. This activity has revealed damaging, toxic, or unhealthy relationships as I've embraced HEART.

If that happened for you as you did this exercise, congratulations. While it may not feel like a victory now, you have all the information you need to salvage your lost energy. Reinvest that energy in your HEART, starting with your physical and emotional needs, and then focusing on the relationships you want to cultivate.

Evaluate My Relationships

Once you know who your people are, it's time to evaluate each relationship according to need.

The demands of each relationship vary based on the duration, intimacy, and history, as well as each individual's unique needs. For example, my husband and I have put years and years of time into cultivating our relationship. We've prioritized each other. Because of that, we have a solid foundation. Relationships take work, but ours doesn't require much.

My kids are a different story. Even though I see them every day (and have been with them since before they were born), our relationship is still being built. These are the years when I put in the time. When I'm tempted to dismiss my kids in favor of work or something else I "have" to do, I remind myself that these relationships take time to build. These are especially important to me right now because, for kids, there's a limited window of time to invest. Their formative years are happening right now. I can't push this off until later.

The truth is, some of our relationships might need restructuring. Some will need more attention, some will need less, and others will need to be eliminated. Others simply need regular maintenance. How do we go about knowing which is which?

To start, I've compiled a list of reflection questions about your concentric circles. You don't have to answer every question, but I would recommend starting with Circle 1. Answering these questions may help you identify issues in one or more of your most important relationships.

- What's working for this relationship? What's not working and needs to be addressed?
- What are you getting out of this relationship? What are you contributing?
- Does the relationship have a rhythm? If so, what is that rhythm and is it working for you?
- How much does this relationship require from you? What is the hopeful outcome?

- How long has this relationship been around and how long do you think it will stay around?
- Is it a relationship that has fallen on the wayside and needs a revamp?
- Is it a toxic relationship that you need to cut out of your life?
- Are the needs of the relationship more than is realistic for you?
- Are you keeping this relationship for what it was or for what it is now?
- Are your needs or the needs of this other person getting met? Why or why not?
- Do you find yourself avoiding or ignoring this person? Why?
- Do you need to say or do anything that hasn't been said or done in this relationship?
- After spending time with this person, do you feel drained or full of energy?
- What is a healthy relationship?

What is the best way to tell when a relationship is working for me and when I should end the relationship?

Breaking up is hard to do. And if not hard, impossible. Some relationships come with burdens. Sometimes it feels like we have a duty-to-a-human, rather than a meaningful relationship. Ask any new mom. As much as she prayed for that bundle of wonder, there were moments in hindsight she questioned her sanity.

Some relationships carry horrific wounds and heavy scars. These injuries may be unfortunate, unforgivable, or unforgettable. It's tempting to numb. Or cower. Or both.

Relationships are fires that refine us.

The struggle is part of the story.

Is there a lesson buried in your difficult relationships? Something to redeem all you lost? Or are losing?

There is always a lesson. And lessons are part of what makes life beautiful. We just have to choose to see them that way—like guideposts.

I know these marks are hard to think of as gifts, but I promise, if you look for the lesson you can find the beauty.

Here's a list I use for each of my relationships. It's a quick way to evaluate whether or not my favorite five are thriving or in need of some work.

I don't get too fixated on these indicators. Like a car dashboard, the fuel tank can get to a quarter tank or less before worry sets in. Oil changes happen about every three months, but if you go a few days over, it won't ruin your car forever. But if you see a blinking red light—especially that fuel light—you need to take notice and pull over as soon as possible.

The same is true with relationships. Armed with your favorite five, think about these eight basic markers of a healthy relationship:

1. We have shared values, interests, and experiences.
2. We have transparency and trust, kindness and respect.
3. We have sensitivity to one another's needs, desires, and emotions.
4. We have teamwork: we encourage each other.
5. We have a balance of give-and-take (it's not always one person doing the work).
6. We have good communication skills and make an effort toward improving.
7. We have mutual loyalty to one another (the connection feels safe).
8. We have love and sexual attraction (for an intimate partnership).

Remember, it is *not* about meeting all of these criteria 100 percent, all the time. Use this list as a standard to assess the strengths and weaknesses of your favorite five relationships.

If you realize your relationships need some work, you're not alone. Relationships change, and it's never too late to begin prioritizing what matters. Here are some things you might discover as you're completing this exercise. See if any of these are for you:

- I'm not maximizing my time with my kids. I need to learn new ways to connect with them.
- I need better boundaries with my extended family.
- I need to attend fewer social events so I can make more space for my immediate family.
- I have let my efforts to contribute to my community take over more important priorities.
- I need more intimate time with my significant other.

- I'd like to stop prioritizing acquaintances over my closest relationships.
- We need to host more social events at our house.

Armed with your favorite five, a hopeful perspective and an eye to see the good and say it, ask yourself how you can maximize those relationships—how can you make those people better and how can they make you better?

Ask, What Can I Realistically Give?

You've identified your people, evaluated your relationships, so it's time to identify what you can *realistically* give to each relationship. Let go of the belief that you have to sacrifice yourself for the sake of your relationships in order to add value. It's enough that you're a friend, daughter, aunt, mother. When you focus on your favorite five, *All Your People* starts to feel life-giving instead of soul-sucking.

What do my people need from me—and can I *realistically* offer it? Our people need from us:

- Time: doesn't have to be intentional, just has to be present
- Engagement: active listening or paying attention
- Intentionality: checking in on a friend that is hurting, remembering birthdays or important events, planning time to connect
- Practical support: dropping off a meal, offering to babysit, running a quick errand, answering a question, helping with homework
- Touch: snuggling, cuddling, hugging, holding hands
- Honesty: communication of boundaries and limits, a hard conversation about a time you were hurt, an apology

We often make life more complicated than it needs to be, don't we? Maintaining a relationship doesn't have to be difficult. We don't have to plan an elaborate girls' trip. It could be as simple as a text message to check in. Building relationships isn't about getting it all done in one day; it's about measured investments over the long haul.

Cultivating relationships takes intention, but the connection is a reward. Take advantage of available opportunities. Compliment people. Text the girlfriend you're thinking about. Call your mom on your way home from work. If it's not something you can do now, schedule it into your day, week, or month. But ultimately, don't overcommit yourself.

KIDS, ETC.

Some relationships don't align with the give-and-take, healthy relationship picture I'm painting here. Kids fall into this category. Kids can be exasperating, but they are our spiritual and legal responsibility. They might frustrate us, test our patience, make us question our sanity, and push our buttons, but relational challenges reveal ways we can grow. Any tricky or taxing relationship can be viewed as a burden or benefit. This might be a difficult parent. A needy coworker. A lonely neighbor. Relationships can help us grow, or help us go. We can't change them, so we best accept them, and better yet love them and the opportunity to serve. Making these choices won't always be easy—and there are many relationships that wouldn't be appropriate to do away with, no matter how frustrating they are.

We recently called off a family vacation. It was the right choice and, after weighing the cost, a simple one to make. But it left our kids' spring break empty. After the trip fell through, we slipped back into the normal routine of stay-at-home days—our kids' school break no different than any other week. It required a conscious decision to take the now-empty time and use it to invest in those important small-circle relationships.

It took intentionality and creativity, but we turned those empty days into time together, small joys, and relational wins. We turned off our phones, ate ice cream for dinner, bought a new board game, lingered over lunch, made popcorn and sprinkled it with cinnamon sugar, and watched movies. We disregarded caloric intake (because that's the actual definition of vacation, amiright?), and one morning "invented" a new recipe by adding things to pancake batter that had never been added to pancake batter before. (If you haven't tried fried jalapeño and cheddar pancake balls, you should.)

I hope that even though we couldn't go anywhere, my kids will remember those moments we spent at home together during the break. The satisfaction of our need and desire for relationship can be that easy. Little actions add up. In fact, sometimes it takes less than thirty seconds.

Anytime I find my priorities out of whack, I ask myself, *What am I hanging on to? What am I refusing to sacrifice or let go of?* Is it time? Aren't relationships worth our time? If it's a coffee date, that's an hour of my time, plus thirty minutes of buffer for transportation. All I must do is coordinate it and then show up. If an hour and a half is too much for a season of life, I can fulfill that friend's request for a coffee date by explaining I have a hard stop and would be happy to do a video call for thirty minutes instead.

We are born with a deep relational need to feel seen and heard and connected. This need cannot be sacrificed on the altar of whatever we deem to be more important. And like the earlier two foundational needs, it does not require a huge investment of time. Little bits of time for relationship, structured into our schedules or captured intentionally throughout our days, add up. And things that add up make a bigger difference in our lives than we often give them credit for.

Investing in relationships can be easy and fun. It's about taking advantage of the little moments with the people we love most. When we prioritize those who matter, using our concentric circles strategy, we take advantage of the small, everyday moments to bring them joy and grow our connection. Over time, our relationships become deep and rewarding.

They become our greatest pride and accomplishment. This is a goal worth achieving.

Give According to My Capacity

One of the guidelines I used when I realized my limited capacity is called the Rule of Ten. I realized I had room for no more than ten meaningful conversations each day. At the time, I had eighteen employees, all reporting to me, and I didn't have time to talk to every single person and also spend meaningful time with each child every day.

One of the days when I tried, I felt like I was going crazy.

So I made a rule that I could only have ten meaningful conversations per day. If I had to give five to family members, I only had five left to give to coworkers or friends. If I hit my wall and the phone rings—with a client or friend who needed something from me—I gave myself permission to admit I was at capacity.

Knowing our *capacity* helps us to truly meet our needs rather than going through default motions.

What do your favorite five need, and how can you realistically meet those needs? Brainstorm a couple of simple actions you could take. Your list might look like this:

1. Play a board game with the kids before bed tonight.
2. Drop off a lasagna for the Smiths on Wednesday.
3. Have a movie-at-home date night with David.
4. Text Emily and ask her how her week has been.

For some of you, making this list is enough. You'll have the list halfway done before you even write the darn thing! For others like me, you need to put a bit more strategy behind the list if you plan to execute the intentions you've set. If that sounds like you, this is important: schedule what you can give *according to capacity.*

Schedule the tasks on your to-do list and calendar.

When you identify what you can give, you've created a task. When you have a task, you can schedule it into your calendar. We'll cover scheduling in the next section of the book. But for now, remember that if you put something on your schedule, you're much more likely to do it. Consequently, you're much more likely to notice when something simply doesn't fit into the finite amount of time and energy you have in a week.

The key word here is *capacity. A* comes after *H* and *E* because *you must care for yourself before you can care for your people.* With my physical and emotional well-being foundations in place, I devote my attention to building beautiful relationships with my husband, David, and our kids, and our extended community.

Circling back, don't forget that you are a finite human being. You have limits; you can't be available for everyone. As you place these tasks on your planner or to-do list, notice when the list is at capacity. Dropping off a lasagna might be a kind thing to do, but if you consistently neglect your own needs (or the needs of your family), you are overcommitted and need to pull back.

And, as much as we might like to spend all day, every day, with our people, we have two Life Segments remaining. Be realistic about your time and energy. Prepare your body and mind, make progress with your people, then turn to your next tasks (more on that in the next chapters).

The concentric circles in the *All Your People* Life Segment help you draw vital boundaries. As contrary as it seems, boundaries enrich our relationships; they help our most treasured relationships to flourish, which will then make your life beautiful.

What is your capacity for nurturing the relationships that matter most? How can you make the most of it?

Write It Down, Make It Beautiful

1. Why are your relationships important to you?
2. Use the diagram included in this chapter to document your concentric circle relationships. Does this look the way you'd like it to? Are there any changes you'd like to see, relationships you'd like to cultivate, or boundaries that need to be set?
3. What relationships are most meaningful? Most important?
4. Do any of your relationships need more investment or even a restructure?
5. Are your relationships emotionally fulfilling? Are any emotionally draining?
6. What is the purpose behind the relationships in the smaller circles?
7. How do you maintain and invest in your relationships?
8. How do you set boundaries in your relationships? Are you comfortable saying no or asking for help when you need it?

9. Who needs an investment infusion? How can you do this realistically?

10. What relationships are in maintenance mode right now? What does that look like?

11. Are there any toxic relationships that make you feel uncomfortable or smothered? What small next step can you take to mentally or physically create distance?

Chapter 7

R–RESOURCES AND RESPONSIBILITIES

"Clutter is the physical manifestation of unmade decisions fueled by procrastination."
CHRISTINA SCALISE[1]

Y ou know that sinking feeling in your gut—the one that tells you there's something important you forgot? I had that feeling a couple weeks ago. It was a Monday morning, and I was making breakfast, reviewing the upcoming week in my head, when it hit me: my gas tank was on empty—and not just eighth-of-a-tank empty; it was fuel-light-came-on-yesterday empty. Having tested the limits of my gas tank before, I knew I was cutting it close.

Normally, this wouldn't be that much of a problem—I'd just need to leave a few minutes early to get gas on the way to school, then head straight to my client meeting. I glanced at the clock as I whisked eggs in a skillet. Still plenty of time, I thought.

That was before my eldest came downstairs with a wrinkled piece of paper in his hand. The top read "Field Trip Permission Slip" and the due date was last Friday. The fee for the field trip was ten dollars, cash.

As they say, the plot thickened. I had used my cash yesterday at the grocery store. I could get more, but it would require a trip to the bank. This meant two stops before school drop-off, or one after—with an extra trip back to school to drop off the form and the money.

It was at this point that our kitchen, perpetually in a state of remodel, tripped me on an electric and plumbing stub, and the plate in my hands went flying, straight into the face of my youngest.

Now I was starting to scramble, the breakfast now strewn through my daughter's hair.

So, when my middle child appeared complaining that he didn't have a shirt for school, it took every ounce of willpower in my being not to come unglued. I had to take a moment. It was a Monday indeed.

We made it to the gas station. We made it to school—a little late (second-day shirt and all). My oldest went on his field trip, my youngest got the eggs out of her hair, and miraculously, I made it to my client meeting on time. But there was a moment of panic when I feared my disorganization would lead to the downfall of our day.

You've been there: a morning (afternoon or evening) that didn't go as planned. It's not quite as discouraging as life not going according to the plan, but still. Minor mistakes multiplied, and, even if none of it was your fault, it fell to you to patch circumstances and offer apologies. Who else was going to manage all those details? The solo-management feeling only compounds the Monday agitation, right?

That morning, with a plate full of blunders (not eggs), I forfeited the image of an ideal day. You've been there too, right? We can all manage the occasional chaotic morning when necessary. But the occasional morning isn't the issue. It's when one morning becomes five mornings in a row—when you can't make progress in other areas because small fires keep popping up. You are distracted from the projects and people you care about because the basics keep falling apart.

Of course, this happens sometimes. It's life. But is it possible to set ourselves up in such a way that this isn't a daily, or weekly, occurrence?

Three Guiding Checkpoints

We are all responsible for *a lot* on a typical day. The bills, unexpected expenses, missing socks, restocking toiletries, an oil change—never mind the logistical gymnastics we perform to schedule family and work commitments. As women, we are capable of so much. Our days and our heads are full of tasks unexciting, but essential for survival, efficiency, and productivity.

Resources and Responsibilities is the place for those pesky little tasks that clutter up our cars, homes, and days.

I find three systems essential—and they will quit working if you don't maintain them regularly: money, car, and home. These three checkpoints can make a big difference in how smoothly your life runs.

Money

The benefit of cash flow, savings, and financial literacy cannot be overstated. Have you ever noticed how having your finances under control allows you to turn your attention to other pursuits, like your career or your family? With a small amount of planning, unexpected expenses like your car insurance renewal don't ruin your month.

Money stress makes it hard to focus on anything else.

Car

No matter how new or old your car is, when you take care of it, it will continue to transport you from one place to the next. Your car gets you to important events like work, school, and church. We know we're doing a good job maintaining the car checkpoint when we don't have to think about it.

Our car is just *there* for us when we need it.

Home

When our homes are clean and organized, our lives are more efficient and effective. It's easier to find the screwdriver, saving the energy it would take to dig through a tool chest, and gifting us with an extra hour before company arrives. An organized home clears up space in our minds and in our days.

The problem is, it's easy for little things to pile up and, rather than being a place of refuge, our home becomes a source of stress and frustration for us. When you fall behind on household duties, catch-up can feel difficult, if not impossible.

When the checkpoints of *Resources and Responsibilities* are maintained, they become invisible.

But if you don't tend to them regularly, they end up disrupting your life in minor emergencies: your tire pops, your AC stops running, or you come up short for the month's bills. Of course, these emergencies can happen even when you're regularly tending to your responsibilities. They're just much less likely to happen. Your productive day (or week or month) can quickly dissolve into chaos when any of the three parts come unhinged.

These three systems are important because they are truly *needs*. Without a grasp on finances, life becomes a month-to-month struggle. Without a safe and orderly home, we suffer emotional, and sometimes physical, consequences. Without transportation, we are limited in what we can accomplish.

It can feel overwhelming to care for so many things. But that's what Resources and Responsibilities is for—to help us manage details so life never seems like too much.

Few of us are financial experts or organizational gurus. Not many of us know much about the mechanics of our vehicles. The truth is, we don't need to be CPAs or mechanics or DIY experts. What we need is basic organization. We need systems and we need a plan.

We will make three lists that will save you hours of energy: financial needs, transportation/vehicle needs, and home/housing needs.

Money

A CPA told me one time, "Good accounting is 95 percent organization," and suddenly, math made more sense. It sounds too simple to be true, right? Simply organize my documents, keep track of information, and this will help me reach my financial ambitions?

Yep.

Financial resources require maintenance and management. If you've ever found yourself in a financial bind (hand raised), you know what it feels like to learn this lesson the hard way. Everyone's financial situation is unique, but whether it's making a budget, adjusting the budget, paying unexpected bills, or planning for future expenses, the financial aspect of our lives requires our full attention.

Without a system in place to steward our finances, we risk running into negative consequences in other areas of our lives.

This isn't a book about budgeting. Thank goodness we don't have to learn (and I don't have to teach) accounting principles to gain control over our finances and improve our lives. Trust me, math is not a prerequisite to a beautiful life, hallelujah. But we do need to craft a *vision* for what our financial life could look like.

We do this by asking: *Where are we now? Where would we like to be?*

FILE BY BINDER HACK

One simple trick that helped me immensely was keeping an "important documents" binder, both in my desk drawer, on my phone, and on my computer desktop. It's not the most advanced form of organization—but everything must have a home. I started with one simple rule: alphabetize everything. When one binder got full, I made tabs and separated the sections into other binders, still alphabetizing everything. Now, when I needed to look up important documents, account information, or insurance policies, I knew where to go. When it comes time to do taxes, I pull everything out of the tax binder. After years of having one binder, my collection is now expanding and I'm looking for a way to create an archive. But it all started very simply: with one binder.

The world of personal finance today is different from the way it has been in the past—both in what people are financially responsible for and in how people get out of debt, save, and achieve financial stability. People work from home, coffee shops, and airplanes. People are self-employed, freelancers, or side-hustlers. Jobs look different these days.

The rules around finances—and the tricks to make sure everything is accounted for—are changing. Figure out what works best for you.

This will take self-reflection, a willingness to try new things (and fail at a few), and a little bit of planning and organization.

First let's talk about *self-reflection*.

Our habits and thought patterns about money are driven by our (often unconscious) beliefs, so we should start with self-reflection. Financial scripts must be acknowledged and addressed. It won't matter what kind of budget or system we use until we figure out *why* we're constantly overspending, obsessively tracking every penny, or failing to meet our charitable giving targets.

Take time to reflect on your feelings about spending, saving, and giving. Identify past experiences with money, your expectations of money, and your vision for what your financial life could look like.

These reflections will help you get on the same page as your spouse or financial partner.

Finances can be stressful—especially when someone shares your bank account. Whatever system you're following, it may seem that the system always seems to fail you or that you're always at odds about this subject. Talk to your spouse, not only about expenses but about how you're feeling about money.

These questions can be used as journal prompts or conversation-starters with your significant other as you reflect on your underlying feelings about money.

- When it comes to money, what emotions do you experience?
- When do you feel these emotions?
- What past experiences have you had with money that feel notable?
- What are nonnegotiable expenses for you?

- Do you have enough to cover the basics?
- What do you both want to spend money on?
- What do you have disagreements about?
- Is there a place for compromise?
- What are your shared values, and how are you putting money toward those values?
- Are you preparing for your future? If so, how?

Second, let's talk about trial and error. It may take some trial *and error* to discover what works best for you when it comes to your finances. I emphasize the "and error" part because you can't expect the system you come up with to immediately solve all of your money woes. This is about figuring out what works for you over the long term. Developing your routine will take time.

Read books. Ask for help from trusted advisors. Find a system that looks good enough and tweak it to work for you and your family. If after a few weeks, a practice you tried isn't helping you, let it go. Let's say you tried the envelope system, for example, and it isn't bringing more peace to your financial life—ditch it. Find something else that *does* work for you.

This is not about finding the one perfect way. It's about putting together a plan that serves you and your family.

Mostly, don't give up. Implementing new financial stewardship habits and routines will take a while. As you take intentional steps in the right direction, know that you are making progress. You're inviting your vision of *what could be* into existence. That is good, hard, and healing work.

Finally, let's talk about organization.

There are three elements essential to organizing your finances. Here is how I organized our finances:

- Expenses
- Preparation
- Planning

I know this is way oversimplified but that's the beauty of it. There is an app for everything and there are far more sophisticated programs out there you can use to get your finances organized, but for the sake of simplicity, let's talk about these three simple steps.

Expenses

Everything has a cost—home upkeep, car maintenance, healthy eating, gym membership, dinner with friends. It all costs money. Are you aware of what your expenses are? Using the questions below, take some time to make a list. You'll be surprised how much relief you find just knowing where you spend.

* What do I regularly spend money on? (Hint: you could go through your bank records or credit card statements for help with this one.)
* What debt do I have?
* What unexpected expenses come up that cause me stress? (My friend Holly once told me she had a sticky note over her computer that read "Teeth. Tires. Taxes.")
* What seasonal events do you need to save for? Do you need to start a slush fund?
* When it comes to unnecessary expenses, what impulse purchases do I always fall for?
* Where am I spending money that I know I'd like to cut back? (Or where would it be realistic to do so?)

Preparation

It is possible to *prepare* for these expenses you brainstormed above. But it does take planning—and planning takes time.

* What information and documents do I need to organize for my finances?
* Have I set up automatic payments or set reminders for expenses?
* Who do I need to talk with about my finances (financial advisor, spouse)?
* How can I continue to educate myself about finances?

Planning

Keeping finances organized isn't just about planning for everyday expenses—although that's a great place to start. It's also about planning for the future, for the *vision* you imagined for yourself and your financial life. Use the questions below to help you think about what the future looks like for you when your finances are under control.

* What am I saving for, and what dollar amount can I afford to save each month?
* When is my *scheduled* time with myself, my partner, or my team to talk about finances?
* Where am I investing in my future?
* How can I continue to do that?
* To whom or what am I *giving*?

Car

Like housing, transportation typically represents a large investment of time and money. Tire rotations, oil changes, washing, gas fill-ups—all that work, but without the satisfaction of a good DIY transformation. It's still the same car.

If I neglect to maintain my car, there can be consequences. You've seen this play out in a comedy. The fuel light comes on, the door handle falls off, the duct tape doesn't hold, and our hero is stranded on the side of the road, engine sputtering and expletives spewing. He coughs up the dough to tow it, and lands in a rental car with an unwelcome (but funny) companion. Dangerous situations arise, someone gets hurt (but it's funny), they miss the train and end up squashed into a crop duster. There's a happy ending, and it's a box office hit.

In reality, we could put ourselves in danger, like the time my car stalled in the middle of an intersection on the way to drop the kids off at preschool.

But you know that.

It's easy to forget the regular maintenance our car needs. It's easy to put off repairs. We don't check the oil. We don't rotate the tires. We forget to change the brake light. These tasks that are so easily pushed to the bottom of our priority lists. Do you know how many cars I've seen with duct-taped windows? Enough to know that I'm not the only one putting off small (or large) repairs.

A little bit of maintenance makes a long-running car. For instance, cleaning out the car. This is something I've put off in the past, and we've ended up with a gross car. With three kids and a dog, the floor mats are covered in sand, stickers, and saliva. Every seat features a stale french fry and enough crumbs for the dog to easily make it a full meal. And I know this is disgusting, but I don't think you can be a mom if you haven't at some point gotten into your car and then promptly out again because you smelled sour milk coming from who knows where. I've noticed something: as the car gets dirtier, the less I care, the more I complain—and want to buy a new one.

I don't need a new car. What I need is to clean the one I have.

An ounce of prevention is worth a pound of cure here. While getting a full car detail can be expensive, cleaning out my car every time I fill up with gas is free. And not to oversell it, this ritual can save the day. Think about this: the next time you get gas, make it fun. Instead of waiting until the last minute to fill up, turn it into a Coke date with yourself. Make a playlist. Go to your favorite gas station at your favorite time of day. Turn up the music, open the doors, and find all the french fries. Instead of making it a chore, make it a moment.

Bonus benefits: less complaining, less frustration, and less humiliation when things don't fall out of my car during school pick-up.

Of course, if you prefer to save for car detailing, just be sure to build it into your budget.

If you don't have a car or share one with family, then you also need to create a strategy for who gets the car when, and how you can make sure you'll have access to transportation when you need it. Either way, this will take some preparation and planning.

- Where are the places you frequently need to go? What do you need to get there?
- What common emergencies/interruptions keep you from getting where you want to go on time? How can you prepare for those?
- What are the weekly tasks that keep you on track?

- Are there any monthly or occasional maintenance responsibilities?
- What can you do to set yourself up for success in transportation?

Home

I could write an entire book on what I love about home. Of all the checkpoints, home is my favorite, simply because it means so much to each of us. And it matters like never before. Home is not only a physical shelter from the elements; it should be a safe place for us to discover who we are.

I want our home to be a sacred space, with doors open wide to welcome weary travelers in need of rest and nourishment. I want it to meet our needs for safety and shelter, but I also want it to touch souls. I want warm lighting and I want to smell rosemary and citrus when I stand in the front yard, the clean scent of clothes in the dryer.

On most days, our homes keep our lives running smoothly, providing what we need at the right time. Need an outfit for the day? It's in the closet. Need moisturizer? It's on the shelf. Need a snack for the road? It's in the cupboard. Need a shower? There's that too. Want to watch a show? There's a spot on the couch made just for that.

But keeping a household running takes maintenance. Taking out the trash, making the beds, watering the plants, doing the dishes, or tidying up toys are incessant chores. Then there are the weekly requirements; grocery orders, cleaning the bathrooms, and maintaining the yard. Seasonal responsibilities could include changing air filters, turning on heaters, removing Christmas lights, and preparing for winter or rain. Whether you own a home or rent, you will need to check in on repairs, replacement of fences and patio covers, and repainting rooms.

For some people, putting a home in order is easy. Some people adore tidying up. They find daily homekeeping tasks rejuvenating. They know when something needs repair (and it bothers them until it's fixed). I am not this person.

I love a well-ordered home but struggle to empty the dishwasher or fold my laundry when more exciting options, like writing a book or painting a piece of furniture, present themselves.

This struggle doesn't make home upkeep any less necessary. If I neglect my home's needs I won't be able to use and enjoy our home in the way I had hoped.

- What are your current feelings about your home? What makes you feel that way?
- What regular maintenance does your home need?
- Who is responsible for that maintenance?
- Is there anything on that list you can automate or schedule?
- What room or section of your house do you avoid? Why?
- What could you do in this part of the house to make it more functional?
- What part of your home often causes you stress or drives you crazy? Is there anything you can do?

How to Face a Full Plate

Based on the three checkpoints—money, car, and home—make three lists. In each list, write down tasks you need to do to keep the *R* in your HEART functioning.

Your lists might look like:

Money
1. Schedule a monthly money meeting.
2. Put taxes on calendar.
3. Balance checking account.
4. Keep coffee money in a separate envelope.
5. Set up automatic 10 percent tithe at church.

Car
1. Schedule oil changes in consistent intervals.
2. Get gas on Sundays at the cheap gas station.

3. Purchase an AAA membership for peace of mind.
4. Pick a month to get tires rotated.

Home
1. Organize my closet so getting ready in the morning isn't so stressful.
2. Come up with a system for getting kids' clothes sorted, donated, or passed to a sibling.
3. Delegate tasks—emptying the dishwasher, taking out the trash, picking up toys.

Assign each task a deadline or frequency. I use the notes pages in my planner to make these lists, and update my lists as I think of new action items.

As a bonus, these lists might also highlight what we *don't* need, which is useful information. For example, one summer I listed out everything it takes to maintain my car, and realized that with my work-from-home lifestyle, I didn't need a car in that season. I could take the kids to their activities in David's car. I spent that summer without a huge (and expensive) piece of equipment sitting in my driveway.

You might find yourself getting stuck in the brainstorming process, or in the actual implementation of the process. Do what you can at the time and try to move forward.

When I keep making the same mistake, I try to automate the process. Is there a way for me to make this happen without thinking about it? Or to schedule in a reminder? The "failure" isn't a failure of will. It indicates that my process isn't working for me. No need to shame myself—it's time to change the process.

The big secret that no one tells you about adulthood is that we're all faking it out here. We're all trying to get by. We're all figuring it out as we go. But by organizing your life, you are more empowered than you thought was possible.

Take a break if you feel overwhelmed with everything on your plate. You can't reflect on your needs while barreling down the highway at ninety miles per hour. Rest. Pause. Journal about what feels unmanageable. Carve out time in your day to tackle this, one topic at a time. It takes as little as thirty minutes. Journaling is an investment in your life, not a sacrifice of your time. It keeps the overwhelm at bay and gives you clarity concerning your tasks.

The first victory is identifying the need. After identifying my needs, I can schedule them in my planner. We'll return to what to do with this in a few chapters when we talk about follow-through.

How Our Resources and Responsibilities Shape Us

Organizing our resources and responsibilities helps us avoid inconvenience and disaster, and can teach us about ourselves and also transform us.

For David and me, personal finances have been unpredictable. I joke that we have a "feast or famine" lifestyle sometimes. The bank account feels full or empty, but rarely in between. At one point, for example, we had a handful of expenses I was not aware of. The lack of communication between us turned into a big financial mess—and an argument.

Calling in reinforcements, we went to see a marriage counselor.

To our surprise, the marriage counselor asked us if we were giving any of our money away. We said no. At that time, we weren't giving financially in any way. We were barely making it. He then suggested that we begin tithing. We quickly assured him that there was no room to cut anything from our budget. I looked him in the eye and said, "We're here because we're broke. Where would we get this money?"

The counselor suggested we begin by giving away 1 percent of our income the first month. Just one. Then 2 percent the second month. Then three. Until we reached 10 percent.

It surprised me, but this was the best financial advice we've ever received. As our generosity to others increased, we became more generous with ourselves, clearer on our values, and willing to work together.

Everything fell into place.

So, part of our plan has become 10 percent giving. We work it into our system. We plan for it. And it changes us, helps us become more giving.

But it's not just the practice of giving that has this power; even something as simple as cleaning up our kitchens can be transformative.

As we care for what we have, we value it more. We use it more wisely and appreciate it more. Instead of our car, house, and finances being sources of chaos and stress, they become opportunities for gratitude. By taking care of our resources, we learn to live in daily appreciation of the basics. As challenges arise and we must change our lifestyle (buy a used car, downsize our home, or tighten up the budget), we learn about what we value and what we can sacrifice. We learn what is important to us.

When we have the courage to face our *Resources and Responsibilities* with care, thoughtfulness, and follow-through, it changes us for the better.

Staying organized isn't a chore; it's an opportunity and pathway to a more beautiful life.

Write It Down, Make It Beautiful

1. What is your vision for the finances portion of your life? What is the current state of your finances? Do you know what your financial needs are, specifically?

2. What is your vision for your home and living space? What does a safe and comfortable home feel like? Do you have any specific or unmet needs in this area?

3. What is your vision for your transportation or vehicle? Do you have any specific need or vision for this part of your life?

4. How often do you review your finances? How often do you need to review them? Do you have a financial road map for your future?

5. Do you ever have any surprise repairs or home issues? How can you prevent those in the future? What could you do today that would prevent chaos tomorrow?

6. You've heard the saying, "messy desk, messy mind." The same goes for our vehicles. Messy car, messy calendar. What could you do weekly or monthly to help maintain your vehicle?

7. What next steps do you need to take to improve your financial position?

8. What next steps do you need to take for maintaining your home space?

9. What next steps do you need to take to maintain your transportation or vehicle?

Chapter 8

T–TRADE AND TALENT

"There is no such thing as work-life balance. Everything
worth fighting for unbalances your life."

ALAIN DE BOTTON

No matter what "work" means for you (volunteer work, selling essential oils, your furniture-flipping side project, your hobby business, that book you're working on, the way-way-more-than-full-time business you started a while back, or a full-on CEO position), we're all looking for the same things when it comes to our employment. We want something that feels meaningful, manageable, and memorable.

The questions we tend to ask ourselves include: *How can I make my highest contribution to my people and community? How can I cultivate my talents and abilities? How can I be of service? Where can I dig in and make a difference?*

And maybe it's precisely because we take our work lives so seriously that we find ourselves getting into trouble.

Several years ago, while running a successful planner business, I decided to take on some friends' interior design projects. At that point I had moved from hand-painting Christmas cards to selling day planners and calendars, and decided it was time to explore a new avenue (enter my longtime passion, interior design).

Things were going well. The volume of planners we were selling was steadily increasing each week and month, while I was also receiving more interior design inquiries than ever before. This was a good thing—right?!

The challenge was, things were starting to feel . . . unsteady.

Imbalanced.

Off.

I couldn't put my finger on it. Nothing was chaotic or out of control yet. I wasn't in the final stages of burnout (like I had been before). I just noticed it didn't matter how many tasks I accomplished in a day, there were always a few thousand more. I didn't feel like I was managing the Trade part of my life very well.

All my other Life Segments were running smoothly in the background. We were remodeling a house—replacing a broken air conditioning unit (a big deal in the middle of an Oklahoma summer) and dealing with fallout from an electric panel upgrade. And on top of everything, I had, for some unexplained reason, committed to paint t-shirts with my kids and the neighbors.

This "unique" set of circumstances might sound pretty familiar. Whether you're homeschooling your kids or making spaces beautiful from the ground up or rescuing old furniture and restoring it to its original beauty or trying to change the way families think about home healthcare or teaching Sunday School or bringing in the primary income for your family—you've thrown your whole heart into it.

You want to make a difference. You want to do something that matters. You don't want to waste your time. In fact, you want to invest your time into something long-lasting. You just don't want to miss the rest of your life in the process.

HEART did exactly what it was designed to do. It brought me back to my core, back to my needs, back to my heart. Not to steal me away from work. But so that I could bring my highest and best self to the table.

The Joy of Work

The *Trade and Talent* Life Segment asks the question, *How do we organize our working hours so that we may contribute our highest and best self to our community?* Giving of our talents, skills, and abilities is part of the beautiful life we long for. How do we *give* without upsetting the precious but precarious balance we have just infused in our lives?

Here's an amazing thing: when the other four Life Segments are in balance, this one is almost unrecognizable from what it was before. When I show up for work (at my desk, with a client, or online) with my life and HEART in order, my work serves me just as much as I serve it. I've just filled my HEART, and I'm not working with a deficit of time, attention, and energy anymore. I show up rested, realistic, empowered to respond confidently to whatever the day throws at me.

My biggest struggle with *T* is that, like kudzu or green ghost slime, it threatens to suffocate everything else. I have to remind myself that if (and when) I let work take over, everything suffers—including my *work*. When my projects are all I'm thinking about, all the time—when I'm heading back to my office after dinner and checking email before breakfast—I'm in the danger zone.

I've repeatedly learned that my life is better when I prioritize the other four letters, putting *T* in its due place; everything functions better. I'm energized, physically and emotionally, my relationships are stable, my home and finances are in (a semblance of) order. With these potential obstacles managed to the best of my ability, I'm poised to handle work projects. And yes, even work *stress*.

When *Trade and Talent* are properly positioned on the priority list, I don't bring less to the table. I bring more. Because I have more to give.

There are times in life when this order is put to the test. When a project at work gets stressful and starts to take over my brain, and I feel myself floundering. When that happens, it's natural for me to neglect the first four Life Segments. That's exactly when I need to lean into HEART.

See if any of these problems sound familiar:

* Staring at a screen instead of typing an email
* Running over the same problems in your head repeatedly with no breakthrough
* Writer's block
* Lashing out at a coworker
* Daydreaming and lack of focus
* Constant interruptions at home
* Falling asleep with your computer open
* Getting to three in the afternoon without any food in your stomach
* Getting to the end of the day feeling terrible about yourself

If this sounds like an all-too-familiar story, consider . . .

* We're wasting our time sitting in front of our computers without making progress because we haven't given our bodies what they need.
* The answers you're looking for aren't "out there" but in your inner world.
* Our conversations with clients and coworkers feel frustrating, hurtful, and unproductive because we haven't emotionally cared for ourselves.
* We're suffering from a lack of focus because there are urgent personal tasks on our minds.
* Because we have neglected our relationships, we don't have the support that would help us succeed.
* Little emergencies interrupt our day and make us less present and productive because we haven't taken care of tasks around the house.

Every day has surprises we aren't responsible for, but when we find ourselves struggling with the emotions that come with an overcommitted schedule, we can choose to set kind boundaries on interruptions. We don't have to sacrifice our working hours to chaos or distraction.

In times like these, I use HEART to recalibrate, reset, and refocus.

When chaos takes the wheel, making it difficult to focus on the work that needs to get done, the only way to regain control is with a HEART reset. Starting at the top, run through the five Life Segments, touching on each checkpoint until you find an action you can immediately take. What is out of sorts? What part of your HEART needs attention *right now*? Here's how I do it, starting at the top:

* H—Help Yourself: Sleep? Water? Nutrition? Movement? Meds?
* E—Empower Yourself: Emotions, Education, Essence? Read, Write, Pray?
* A—All Your People: Who do I need to connect with?
* R—Resources and Responsibilities: What's not taken care of?
* T—Trade and Talent: Is there anything I can do to make quick progress here?

The secret to using HEART for a reset is in finding quick, actionable things that you can do to build momentum into your day. We're not trying to do anything drastic; we're trying to build a progress snowball. Here are a few action steps that help me in the middle of a chaotic workday:

* Make a list. When little emergencies or tasks threaten to interrupt work hours, write them down. The list will do the remembering for you, and you will feel less compelled to stop everything.
* Walk around the block. Nothing calms me better than the rhythm of walking. A change in scenery and fresh air clear my head.
* Get some food. When I feel the chaos of the day overtaking my work hours, I often realize I haven't eaten in hours. I can't always drop everything to go make a healthy meal—and I'm usually too frustrated to cook anyway. Leaving the house or going next door to a coffee shop gives my mind a break and energizes me quickly. Maybe for you, cooking something at home is soothing. Either way, when you're stuck at work, check in to see if you've made time to nourish yourself.

- Take a shower. Showers are the place for getting the ideas flowing—even if this tried-and-true method doesn't produce any groundbreaking insights, your body will feel better and that makes a difference.
- Run an errand. This is a bit of a mind trick, but sometimes I need distraction from a task to restart my brain. As a bonus, I check a long-lingering task off my list.

Maybe I need to make that walk around the block a jog around the neighborhood. Maybe I need to have a quick conversation with David, to make sure we're on the same page about something that's been bothering me. Maybe I need to stop and call the plumber. I manage what's necessary, and then I return to my work.

It might feel like a detour, but it isn't; it's the path in front of you. As you make it a habit, your focus will improve because the important parts of your life are stabilized. Your prior self-care and soul-care efforts have equipped you to cope with the pressure, emotions, and interpersonal interactions that come with working life. Fewer fires will interrupt your day.

It's a moment of reset, but you can't solve all your H, E, A, and R problems in one morning. But sometimes making a quick list of what *needs* to be done frees your brain to get back to the job at hand. Your capacity is your judgment call, but it's a call I'm confident you can make: touch on all five segments, and you are headed in the right direction.

We go further, faster, when we call an intermission to identify and satisfy our needs.

Then, you can focus. And that's where SMART goals come back into the arena.

A Place for SMART

When it comes to *Trade and Talent*, I must admit that SMART goals may be useful, despite my reservations. SMART goals were invented for business and big projects, and the concept serves well in those arenas.

Work backward from where you want to be. Divide the work into manageable tasks. Specify what you need to do and when.

Think about your next project (or whatever your work entails) strategically:

- What are you aiming to accomplish? When does it need to be accomplished by?
- How far can you see into the future? End of your current project? End of the month?
- What do you need to accomplish by that time? What have you already committed to doing? (Choose three goals.)
- Are the goals manageable? What are the advantages of finishing this accomplishment on time? Are there consequences for putting it off? Is there something you need to say no to?
- Divide the goals into smaller tasks. Give those tasks deadlines.
- Schedule these tasks in your calendar.
- Is there space in your schedule to accomplish more? What else can you accomplish?

Your work goals will depend on your type of work and what your role is. Volunteers, employees, and business owners have different needs for their goals. Maybe you're assigned tasks daily—your goals are set for you. Maybe you have set responsibilities as an employee—you want to better your department or meet your goals. Business managers are focused more on developing the company and turning a profit.

SMART goals were designed for business, and, in this context, they help. When given the space and time, this way of attacking your goals gives you focus and direction.

SMART goals will give you focus, but staying focused is another challenge. What keeps a person focused will vary with personality, temperament, and project type. I won't tell you how to go about your work, but I'm all for sharing tactics. As you gather your list of workday to-dos, here are some ways I stay focused and productive even during a long day.

Don't be afraid to say no.

By now, this refrain should sound familiar: this is like a needs-based approach in that it starts from reality. Your time and energy are limited. Feeling ambitious? It doesn't matter how much you *want* to do. You might want to finish an old project, launch a new one, or take on more responsibility, but you can only accomplish so much. By trying to do everything, we prevent ourselves from achieving anything.

When I take on too many clients, projects, or ideas, I get in over my head. I stop following up with the clients I've already taken on. And I (and my team) realize we've got to start saying no.

For some of us, *no* feels like a bad word. We feel guilty saying no, like we should be superhuman—we hold ourselves to an impossibly high standard. As we learn to focus on what we need to do, *no* comes more naturally.

Avoid emergencies by refining your processes.

Process, not workload, is a major component of our chaos. For example, we didn't have a client management system when we started my interior design firm. Slowing my progress, I dealt with each client on a case-by-case basis. As inquiries increased, so did my stress and anxiety. It became clear I couldn't provide a fantastic customer experience without prioritizing organization.

Instead of fighting to keep up, I focused on creating a structure for our processes.

Though it seems counterintuitive, this redirection of energy can solve multiple problems for your future self. What it costs you in the moment, it saves you in the end.

Resist the temptation to panic.

When one part of work feels stressful (not enough money, too many customers or clients, not enough time), everything else starts to feel urgent. I feel a bit of desperation—that's the sign of a scarcity mindset. When it feels like there's not enough to go around, panic sets in, and I throw all kinds of solutions and ideas against the wall, just to see what sticks. I'm willing to try anything to get results. Sometimes this works out, but most of the time, it derails me. It dilutes my remaining resources.

These are my tips, but my guess is that you've been doing what you do long enough to know what works for you. Try making a list of focus tactics. What keeps you on track? Try posting it at your desk or wherever you work: remind yourself to practice what works for you.

Two Questions That Drive Your Work

Theologian Frederick Buechner said, "By and large a good rule for finding out is this: the kind of work God usually calls you to is the kind of work (a) that you need most to do and (b) that the world most needs to have done. . . . The place God calls you to is the place where your deep gladness and the world's deep hunger meet."[1]

I couldn't agree more. In fact, in case it helps, I've divided Buechner's sentiment into two questions. Use these questions as a reflection tool as you consider the best ways to get your work life in balance.

1. Are you helping others with your talents?
2. Are you pursuing your dreams?

As we cultivate our work life, can we push ourselves to connect our skills and passions to serve a need? That's the sweet spot. How have I used my gifts to serve my people and my community? If you can check that box every day, then you are on the right track—and, frankly, you're ahead of most of the world.

But this is not only about helping others with your talents. It's also about *moving toward your dreams*. Because your dreams, in my estimation, are not there arbitrarily. Our dreams have been placed in our hearts so we can bring our greatest gifts to our communities. This is what Buechner is talking about when he says "deep gladness."

Answering these two questions might not make you the most money or get you to the top of the corporate ladder. But the life you live will fulfill you more than any paycheck or title ever could.

When we develop skills and then apply them to opportunities, experience is its own reward. We feel accomplished because we helped. We guided. We made it happen. We provided a solution. Sometimes this happens on a team, and we have the added benefit of celebrating with a group. And when people are grateful for your work, that's even better.

Neither business ownership nor employment is required for this to apply. *Trade and Talent* is anything that uses our skills, gifts, and assets. It could be a hobby. It could be volunteer work. I know that being a homeroom mom is a demanding responsibility. It could be something you do on the side or for fun. I know plenty of people who take on photography projects or challenge themselves to learn a new language or work on their craft. Ask yourself where you feel like you are contributing. Are you a Sunday school teacher? Do you organize events? Maybe you're the Girl Scout troop leader. *Trade and Talent* gives us a sense of purpose and joy.

But as we know all too well, employing our gifts, skills, and passion can also come with stress.

We make a big mistake when we use stress as an excuse to rearrange the order of the Life Segments, our priorities. Although it's tempting to believe otherwise, *T* belongs last. Not only will you perform better, but you'll build a life around what benefits you in the long run.

Work is important. But prioritizing work ahead of our physical and mental and emotional health, our relationships, and our responsibilities is a recipe for disaster. Quality of life—a much more beautiful life—happens when our goals are aligned with our mental, spiritual, and physical health, not with our work ambitions. To maintain balance and quality of life, we need to prioritize our needs and let the rest of life fall into place around those priorities.

Write It Down, Make It Beautiful

1. What is your vision for the *Trade and Talent* portion of your life?
2. How does your trade add value and meaning to your life (helping financially, creating purpose, allowing for a passion project)?
3. Do you ever prioritize career, job, or work over the other Life Segments? How does this cost you?
4. When your *Trade and Talent* Life Segment is in balance with the others, what will that look like?
5. What are your current *Trade and Talent* projects?
6. Do you feel like you're spending too much time or not enough time in *Trade and Talent*?
7. What are the signs for you that *Trade and Talent* is overstepping its role as fifth in HEART?
8. Take a hard look at everything you're doing in the *Trade and Talent* Life Segment. What causes the most stress? What never seems to get done?

9. What brings your focus back to *Trade and Talent*?

10. Do you have a routine that acts as an opening and closing ritual for the time you spend on *Trade and Talent*?

11. What are the next steps you need to be focusing on for *Trade and Talent*?

12. Do any of your *Trade and Talent* projects need to be split into more manageable chunks? If so, list them here.

13. How can you track those goals? If you don't like tracking goals, is there another way you can check in with yourself on those projects, like journaling or meeting with an accountability partner?

14. Be honest with yourself about what you're trying to achieve in *Trade and Talent*: Is it too much? What is "enough"?

PART III

Chapter 9

THE POWER OF YOUR HEART

"Routine, in an intelligent man, is a sign of ambition."
W. H. AUDEN[1]

Now that you've been introduced to HEART and the Life Segments, it's time to put these concepts into action. Remember when I taught my children to ride their bikes? They had to *believe* they could ride (vision), pick a point on the horizon (focus), and pedal (action). With vision and focus but no action, there was no way to balance. Balance demands action.

Or, another way to say this is that if you get excited about a new framework but it doesn't impact your everyday habits and behaviors, I haven't done my job.

Let's implement a practical plan to automate repetitive tasks and systematize your habits. This is the way HEART becomes second nature. After some initial practice, HEART takes almost zero effort. I barely have to *think* about what to do next. When life gets hectic, the framework takes over. When I do things right, in the correct order, I'm moving away from head goals and back to a balanced and beautiful life.

You won't be there yet. But this chapter will get you a few steps closer. Trust the process.

Three Steps to a One-Page Plan

It's time to review the questions you've answered in the earlier chapters. It helps me to rewrite them all on one sheet of paper at this point. You can continue to use the space provided in the book, if you'd like. Notice how the Life Segments have organized your lists!

Now, if you've never tried HEART before, stick with me here. Pause. Acknowledge yourself. It feels impossible to *put on paper* and yet you—miraculous *you*—have been holding these tasks and responsibilities *in your own brain* for heaven knows how long. As overwhelming as it feels to put them on paper, know that once they're out, you'll feel a huge sense of relief.

If your lists don't feel complete in your first sitting, that's normal too. With time, you will discover more tasks and needs and ideas. Add them to your list when you think of them. These lists are meant to evolve. Just because you write something down doesn't mean you're married to it. It's okay to change your mind, take items off a list, or add new ones.

If you're still feeling stuck, I created some example lists below, based on my own experience with HEART. Start with these samples and we'll be on our way.

	GOAL IDEAS:		
	NEED MORE UNINTERRUPTED WORK HOURS.	T	W
♡	I'D LIKE TO GET IN MORE STEPS DAILY.	H	D
	I'D LIKE TO HAVE A DATE NIGHT ONCE A MONTH.	A	M
	I'D LIKE TO READ MORE BUT SPEND LESS ON BOOKS.	E/R	D

If you've skipped the last five chapters, you're probably confused. Take several minutes to answer the questions at the end of the earlier chapters. If you've done that, making these lists is easy (would you expect any less in the *action* section of the book?). Meaning, don't *think* about making the lists. Don't *wonder* about making the lists. Don't make lists in your head. Get out an actual piece of paper and make the *real, actual* lists of needs, responsibilities, and tasks for each of your five Life Segments.

Have the lists in front of you? Good. If you're an overachiever and have rewritten the lists into one consolidated list, even better.

Step 1: Sort and Organize

Use the legend below to rapid-fire assign a time frame to each item. How frequently does each task on the list need to be performed? Does it need to be done daily, or is it something that happens weekly? What needs monthly maintenance? What should happen once a quarter? How about only once a year?

Time Frame Legend:

- D = Daily
- W = Weekly
- M = Monthly
- Q = Quarterly
- Y = Yearly
- LT = Long Term
- 1x = One Time

I like to think of each of these time intervals as "buckets." Before we move on, look at each of your "buckets" and reflect. Do the tasks in your daily bucket encompass all you do, or need to do, on a daily basis? This is a great time to add additional tasks or items if you think of them. I also want to reiterate it's fine to do this rapid-fire. Don't stress. There is no perfect list. Everyone's lists of goal ideas will be unique to them.

A quick note about the "one time" bucket and the "long term" bucket. The "one time" bucket is for nonrecurring maintenance tasks—one-and-done, but must-be-done tasks: chaperoning a field trip, seeing your dermatologist, or hosting a graduation party, for example.

The "long term" bucket is for tasks associated with nonurgent needs, dreams, or even desires. Things that might happen, might not, don't have any specific timeline, and cannot be done anytime soon. Buying a house or a car, moving closer to family, or having a baby. These tasks won't happen within the year and are, in large part, out of your control. *Trade and Talent* is here so that you have a place to put what's in your mind while also realizing that the timeline might shift.

With your needs categorized by time frame, let's move on to the next step.

Step 2: Putting It on the Goal Grid

Meet the Goal Grid. This is a one-page tool to help you see all your goals (ambitions, tasks, whatever you want to call them) in one place. You've put in the work of thought (and handwriting!) and this is where it all comes together. All of that information you've been writing in one handy, easy-to-reference, single-page document. This is the stuff my dreams are made of, guys.

Like your lists, your Goal Grid is unique. Depending on the individual, your completed Goal Grid might look empty in spots. This is neither good nor bad, but it will make you think. Does your daily routine need strengthening? Do you need to be scheduling your months or weeks differently to achieve your dreams?

Before we move on to step three, let's look at how the Goal Grid helps us address activities that fall within each time frame.

Daily Routines

I haven't always been good with routines.

When I was in college, I spent a day mapping out the perfect plan for my daily and weekly life. Gridlines on notebook paper was the original bullet journal, and my hand-drawn schedule reflected the best intentions: study, work, exercise, class. I took it to work the next day and showed it to Rosita, an agent in the real estate office where I worked the front desk. Glasses hanging on

	H	E	A	R	T
LONG TERM	SPA DAY		EUROPE TRIP — KIDS PIANO	TIRES NEXT YEAR	
YEARLY	MEDICAL: PHYSICAL DENTIST DERM.	SOLO RETREAT	TRIP W/ DAVID — FAMILY VACATION	HOA MTG.	TEAM RETREAT
QUARTERLY	TRY A NEW HEALTHY RECIPE — REFILL RX		YES DAY	AIR FILTERS ICE MACHINE OIL CHANGE	TAXES
MONTHLY	MANICURE HAIR APPT		DATE NIGHT	RECYCLING LOG MILEAGE TAX DOCS.	TEAM MEETING —MARKETING —WEBSITE BUFF SHOP
WEEKLY	SLEEP IN — BARRE X 2 — MEAL PREP	CHURCH — PODCAST — MEDITATION	FAMILY DINNER — CALL MOM FAM. PIC.	CLEAN HOUSE — BILLS — MEDITATION	TIMEBLOCK — WEEKLY REVIEW
DAILY	WALK WATER	READ WRITE PRAY	ENGAGE W/ EACH KID & DAVID	LIBRARY CARD — 10 MIN. TIDY	—EMAIL —WRITE —DRAW —DESIGN

the tip of her nose, she studied it. I was basking in the glow of my efforts until she looked over the edge of her glasses and asked, "Aren't you supposed to be rollerblading right now?"

That was the day I learned: we can put all the tasks on the planet in our planners, but that doesn't guarantee they'll magically be completed. Up until that moment, I believed that a plan was enough. Now I know that it takes vision, focus, *and* action to love this beautiful life. The best way to tackle everyday tasks is to make them part of regular routines: a stack of habits that don't require me to think (much) about them at all.

If you find yourself planning or talking about things, but not taking action on them or getting them done, resist the temptation to discount yourself. Let me show you two tricks I learned.

The key is to start with something you already do. Do you eat breakfast every morning? Brush your teeth? Have coffee? Do you pray, meditate, or journal right when you wake up? Start with existing habits. The smaller the better: it just needs to be something you know you'll do.

To develop a routine, hitch a simple task to an existing habit. Last year, adult acne plagued me. As a strategy to improve my face-washing habits, I took something I always do (go to the bathroom in the morning), and added face-washing to build a routine.

I call this habit stacking.[2] For example, drinking a glass of water before and after your morning shower or setting a full water bottle by your bed before falling asleep could help you consume more water. In *The Power of Habit*, Charles Duhigg calls these *keystone habits*. Intentionally tie a drink of water to a daily task, and you'll build a routine.[3]

The second trick is to split the new habit into smaller steps. Adding rollerblading to my routine was too much. I had to remember to schedule the time, put the rollerblades in my car, drive to the lake, and make time for a shower after. My efforts at college scheduling were too haphazard. If I could give advice to my former self, I would have said to start by blocking off the time to rollerblade. Keep chopping until each task feels effortless. Build from there.

Perhaps you want to start running regularly. Pick a routine you already have—drinking a morning smoothie. Then, pick a small task—putting on running shoes after you make your smoothie. Don't make yourself go anywhere. Just put on your shoes. Once you can do that for a week, aim to go outside and stretch. Then, after a week, add walking around the cul-de-sac or the block. Once that's a habit, move to jog the same portion. Soon enough, you're exercising each day.

This might sound like mind tricks—and it is. Your mind is powerful—use it! You already have so many unconscious habits. It's the perfect way to create new ones.

Soon enough, you'll notice that you have a stack of habits strung into a routine. I use morning and nighttime routines, lumping as many tasks as possible into those two time slots. Batching these activities transforms them into a series of automatic actions I don't think about or schedule; they are simply things I do daily.

When you make your nightly routine, ask yourself: What can I do the night before? There's no time like the present to pacify tomorrow's fires.

So, put out the dog's leash or start a load of laundry. We have our kids lay out their school clothes, pack their backpacks, and prepare their lunches. Review your calendar, make an itinerary, clean out your purse, gather supplies for a project, or finalize meals for the next day.

Think of the possibility: *What will this allow for in the morning?* Less stress, more sleep, happier family, smoother commute, healthier choices. You can truly *help yourself* (H) when you're not thinking about what you're doing; you're simply doing it. This is the magic of daily routine. You'll be so much more prepared to handle the day.

When I was starting to incorporate HEART as a daily practice, one thing I did was a run-through of the twelve checkpoints. This quick activity gave me a way to not only check in daily with my long-term goals but also to ensure I was doing the daily things necessary to get me to my long-term goals. With my daily needs met and tasks accomplished, I could better stay on track with bigger-picture goals.

These twelve checkpoints correspond with each of the Life Segments. These single words are prompts to remind me what my needs are:

Sleep
Water
Nutrition
Movement
Heart
Soul

Mind
People
Finances
Home
Car/Transportation
Work

For each item, I list what needs to be done next. It's a rapid-fire exercise, and it refocuses my attention on small steps. Small steps add up to big progress. It helps me stop spinning in a circle by giving me concrete actions that meet my needs and move me forward.

Try it—the practice of the twelve checkpoints relieves us of having to keep everything in our heads all day. When you need a reset, run through HEART, making a list of what you have done and could do for your needs at each checkpoint.

Part of my morning routine is a few minutes of journaling. I always journal something, even if it's just "I'm not sure what to journal right now, so I'll just write about what I need to get done today." Other times, I'll rewrite yesterday's list, adding words for how I feel about the task next to each item. Sometimes putting a feeling beside each word is enough to help me process what I'm up against, emotionally, for the day.

Sometimes I make an effort to work out in the morning. I know people have different views on this, but if I don't get moving in the morning, it might not happen at all. If I squeeze an afternoon workout into an out-of-control day, it will only get half the attention and energy I could have given if I had done it first thing.

I wish I could tell you I have the universally perfect morning and evening routine. But routines are not one-size-fits-all. Waking up at a particular time, eating a certain way, or working out for a certain amount of time cannot guarantee a routine's success. Part of the magic is that routines are the sum of smaller pieces. Everything works together, empowering you in the way of your needs.

Get creative with your schedule. Experiment with times and routines. Build a habit stack that works for you. However you do it, try building these practices to accomplish your daily tasks.

A MORE BEAUTIFUL LIFE

As you fill in your Goal Grid, you'll see some weekly tasks that could be consolidated into one day. For my weekly tasks, I like to designate a "prep day" or a specific day of the week to knock these tasks out. Many people like to use Sunday for this, but I've found that different days can work just as well, if not better. I keep my Mondays and Fridays open as buffer days: Mondays to get started, Fridays to wind down. It's not that I don't work on anything those days (I mean, who *never* works?), but I don't schedule appointments.

A prep day, or weekly review day, has two functions: (1) to plan for the week ahead and (2) to prepare by getting the errands and shopping out of the way. Whatever day you pick for your weekly day, start with about an hour planning time. Reflect on the past week and prepare for the upcoming one.

First, I reflect on the past week:

* How was my sleep, water, and nutrition?
* How was my heart, soul, and mind?
* Were there any relationship issues that came up?
* Did I encounter or overcome any hardships in my finances, home tasks, or transportation?
* How did work go this past week?
* What could I do differently next week?

Then I reflect on the week at hand:

* How can I help my physical well-being this week? (Maybe that means earlier bedtime, more water, more salads, or scheduled workouts.)
* How can I practice empowering myself? Can I carve out time to write, read, or pray? Can I listen to positive podcasts and sermons during a commute?
* How can I practice healthy relationships this week? What conversations do I need to make time for?

- How can I be responsible for my resources this week? What can I do today to make this week go more smoothly? I use my weekly review session to look over budgets or review spending. I will wash the car, update the honey-do list, or take the time to patiently coach my kids on folding and putting away laundry.
- How can I make progress with work this week? What will move the needle for my business or career? What can I do this week that will make money in the future?

Compare your list with your calendar. Then, schedule it in:

This week I will work out one day at 1 p.m.
I will focus on reading and writing to keep my mindset strong, with an hour dedicated to that each afternoon.
I will cook dinner and get a school routine in place for my children on Sunday night. I will wash my car on Tuesday morning.

After I schedule for the week, I prepare for it with practical tasks: instead of work appointments (which I try not to schedule on my prep day), I keep my calendar clear for meal prep, shopping, and other errands.

For me, it's the weekly stuff that slips through the cracks. I forget to take the time to reflect, or I fail to schedule the tasks, and then suddenly, my week feels out of control. It's the meal-prepping, doctor's appointments, and school-night activities that seem to either overtake my day or get lost in the shuffle. I end up asking myself if I accomplished anything at the end of the night.

But it doesn't have to be this way. Prep days help me know exactly when to do what task to help my week go from chaotic to beautiful.

Monthly and Quarterly Batch Days

My best advice for accomplishing monthly and quarterly tasks is to pick a day to batch tasks. Batching is a simple practice. First you pick a calendar day—a get-it-done day. By batching these tasks into one day each week, I'm less likely to forget or lose them in the shuffle.

For monthly tasks, a get-a-lot-done day is one day each month when you get all the monthly stuff done. Some people like to do the first Sunday of the month or the first day of the month, but do whatever works best for you. Treat yourself to a yummy coffee while paying the bills or catching up on budgeting and financial stuff. Make date night dinner reservations. Call your long-distance friend or family member. The point is to batch all those once-a-month tasks into one day each month when you can knock them all out together.

Bills must be paid. A forgotten invoice is a pain point. One day, frustrated with my inability to track everything, I gathered all my bills and rearranged them to be due as close as possible to the same date. It worked best to pick days close to the beginning of the month. By grouping all our bills, I save time (and worry) on our weekly bills.

On monthly get-it-done days, I take stock of the cabinet snacks. I forage for a new, healthy recipe to introduce to my kids. I text old friends, if I haven't heard from them in a while. Even if it can't happen right away, I use that time to schedule it. I schedule a date night.

Repeat this process for quarterly and yearly tasks: assign a quarterly get-it-done day and an annual get-it-done day. Our family quarterly task list includes chores like changing the air and fridge filters, dusting the baseboards, changing the oil, and any seasonal jobs. Yearly tasks for our family include doctor's appointments and tax preparation.

But not everything can be batched. For instance, many of my yearly tasks are attached to holidays. Once a year (around Christmas), I connect with distant friends and relatives. Maybe you volunteer as a family around Thanksgiving or take a family summer vacation in July. When events have specific dates, put them in your calendar as soon as you think of them.

This brings us to your next task: transferring goals from buckets to your calendar.

Step 3: Put It in Your Planner

Decide what to put into your planner. For me, the daily routines are too much to rewrite every day. That stuff lives on sticky notes on my bathroom mirror until it lives in my head. I have one labeled *Morning Routine* and one labeled *Evening Routine*. Maybe you keep this on your Notes app on your phone. Perhaps you keep it by your coffee maker.

Comparatively, weekly and monthly tasks live in my planner.

First, I pick a prep day for the week and mark it in my calendar. On that day, I schedule meal prep, budget review, and other tasks to be done once a week.

I find it's helpful to stay broad and general for monthly, quarterly, and annual tasks. If I get too specific, I'm pigeon-holing myself into a corner where I might end up finding that failure feeling. I don't schedule hour by hour; these calendar days are often too far out. My calendar helps me choose those get-it-done, batching days.

One-time tasks take little reflection. Ask yourself: How urgent is each task? How much time will it take? Can I finish them all in one day? When can I carve out time to get them done?

It is important to schedule one-time tasks. As always, the trick is moving these from the list to the calendar. If you don't schedule them, there's a big chance you'll forget them or be distracted by other matters.

Instead, ask:

- What is one thing I can do today?
- What are two things I can do tomorrow?
- What are three things I can do next Tuesday?

Write it all in your planner. Set the reminders on your phone. Get a journal, a favorite pen, a favorite mug. A favorite water bottle (splurge a little—get a cute one) to keep you hydrated.

Don't give a second thought about when you're supposed to do what tasks. Don't waste a minute deciding what needs to be done today and what can be pushed off until tomorrow—no need to waste energy worrying if everything has been accounted for.

Write It Down, Make It Beautiful

1. Fill out your Goal Grid included below. These buckets may only need a daily or weekly response. Some may only be annually or one-time.
2. Consider your daily tasks that don't need to be put in your calendar but must be done

consistently. Can you create a morning and evening routine that checks off all daily tasks?

3. Gather a list of what you need to do every day. Which of these tasks belong in the morning? Which belong in the evening?

4. What's something you already do every morning that you can build into your morning routine?

5. What's something you already do every night that you can build into your evening routine?

Morning Routine:

Wake up time:

_____

_____

_____

Evening Routine:

Bedtime:

_____

_____

_____

_____

Designate your prep days for weekly, monthly, quarterly, and annual tasks and put them in your calendar:

Weekly:
Monthly:
Quarterly:
Annual:

Chapter 10

IS THIS THING BROKEN?

"If I accept you as you are, I will make you worse; however, if I treat you as though you are what you are capable of becoming, I help you become that."

JOHANN WOLFGANG VON GOETHE

In teaching and using HEART, I've heard a frequent sentiment: Is this thing broken? I hear from people who have learned the framework, understood the concepts, and made the lists. The potential life transformation is exciting. But when it comes to *putting ideas into action*, nothing changes.

Have you ever tried to listen to your heart, but it won't speak? Or it's not speaking loud enough to be heard over the noise of your anxiety, the frenzy of daily life, or your rude inner critic?

If this is you, you're normal. You're not crazy. Your HEART isn't broken (and neither is the framework). But to get those insights and lists to turn to follow-through and action, we need to go a bit deeper.

Once upon a time, a plastic surgeon specialized in face reconstruction, correcting facial deformities and scars. His patients saw him for different reasons. Some of them had been in accidents. Some were born with facial deformities. The outcome of their surgeries startled the plastic surgeon. Many of these patients had become self-conscious around others and repairing their faces didn't always restore their self-esteem. Some struggled to accept their new appearance and felt self-conscious, while others felt more confident and happier. The plastic surgeon asked himself why.

Why did some people's self-confidence improve, and others didn't?

The plastic surgeon discovered something psychologists call the cognitive behavioral model.[1] This is fancy language for self-image. Our thoughts affect how we *see* ourselves, in turn affecting how we *feel* about ourselves, and those feelings ultimately affect—you guessed it—our *actions*.

The bottom line: until we get our self-image in order, our *actions* are unlikely to change.

How to Change Your Self-Image

Self-image is created by self-perception. Self-perceptions come from early experiences, achievements, and failures. It helps me to picture two of me, standing side by side, in my mind. One of those is who I *actually* am, and one of those is who I *think* I am. Turns out, our brain is constantly working to close the gap between these two images. Our brain wants our actions, emotions, behaviors, and talents to *match* our self-image. But if our behavior isn't consistent with our self-image, we usually try to change our emotions, behaviors, and actions—*not* our self-image.

But here's the secret: it's easier to change your self-image than your actions, and if you change your self-image, your actions will change.

Consider the implications: If your self-image doesn't match your actions, you don't naturally change your self-image. That's not the human default. The human default is to attempt to modify our actions. If your self-image is, "I'm a night owl—I've always been that way," don't expect to go to bed early and wake up in time for a workout before your morning routine. Your actions must match your self-image.

In fact, the plastic surgeon I mentioned earlier noticed that, after surgery, patients who had *always* had a healthy self-image felt that their physical appearance had been restored to match their self-image. These patients experienced an emotional recovery as well as a physical one.

The surgeon found that the self-image of patients who had dealt with long-term rejection, embarrassment, or other emotional trauma could not be changed by surgery. The self-image remained unchanged. Even when their physical appearance changed, their perception of themselves remained the same. Some of these patients insisted the deformity remained, and their self-consciousness lingered.

Did you catch that? The deformity was gone, but as far as these patients were concerned, they looked exactly as they had always looked. They felt, acted, and moved through life as someone who remained deformed.

You act in the manner of the person you believe you are.

Is Your Self-Image Holding You Back?

It occurred to me after developing HEART that I needed to exercise more. If there's one checkpoint of any Life Segment that I struggle with, it's that one. I resolved to jog around the block every day. I bought new running shoes—I even put them on in the morning—but after about a week and a half, I stopped. It felt hard. Not to do, necessarily, but to start. If I was honest, I felt like an imposter.

This idea simplified running for me: to become a person who regularly jogs, I needed to *first see myself as a person who regularly jogs.*

All I knew was the Whitney who stayed home and hated running. Jogging Whitney—that was someone I didn't know. I had a hard time following through the Life Segments because my identity was stuck in the past. There's a big difference between pretending to be someone you're not and believing that you're living into your future self.

We all have a self-image in our heads—a picture of ourselves, who we are, and what we look and feel like. That self-image is a rubber band; any time our actions deviate too far, our habits will snap us back to that self-image. We find it difficult to start new hobbies or finish current projects. We all have a self-stereotype and programming that tells us what we are supposed to be.

This is why goal-setting can be so discouraging. Traditional goal-setting methods use comparison goals, tasking us to compare our actual selves—the ones we know well—with other people, who we presumably perceive *differently* than we perceive ourselves. These people run marathons, make millions of dollars, and have every spice in their cabinet labeled and alphabetized. We might seek to be like that person, but unless we believe we *are* like her, we won't change. And being like her isn't what we really want, anyway.

If our self-perception doesn't change, neither do our actions.

Want to know what got me from a person who "hates running" to "a runner"? Want to know what got me from seeing myself as "just not a good texter" to "the friend who reaches out"? Want to know the trick that got me to go from "someone who doesn't open up" to "someone who goes to therapy"?

It's time to visualize.

Why Visualization?

I've talked about the need for vision, the belief that you can live a beautiful life. I haven't yet gotten practical about how you *create* that belief and vision for yourself. To do that, we'll use an exercise called visualization.

Call it the mind's eye, or the theater of the mind: visualization is an effective tool to help us modify our self-image. Victor Frankl credits vision for carrying him through the hell of a concentration camp during World War II. Even in the depths of despair, he *pictured himself* (that's visualization) presenting a lecture in a university setting about the psychology of the concentration camp. It was enough to keep him going in the middle of what felt like hell.[2]

If a vision can help someone survive a concentration camp, that's powerful. Mental imagery has long been used by top athletes to enhance performance. If it's good enough for top athletes and victims of extreme abuse like Frankl, it is also a tool we can use to enhance our lives. Visualization helps us prepare for obstacles, process information, and shift our mindsets. Understanding how our brains use this tool can help us solve problems, overcome fears, and uncover the path to beautiful living.

Turns out, our visual thoughts produce the same mental instructions for our bodies as physical actions. This means mental imagery impacts many cognitive processes in the brain: motor control, attention, perception, planning, and memory. Visualization as a mental practice has been shown to boost motivation, confidence, self-efficacy, and motor performance; prime the brain for the best possible outcomes; and increase flow states.[3]

Humans process information visually. It's easier to file and store that way—a picture is worth a thousand words, right? When we visualize, we communicate with our brains—specifically the lizards in the amygdala—in the language our subconscious understands best.

Think of visualization as a way to communicate with your lizards. If we use our conscious minds to create an *imagined* experience and send the picture to the lizards, they understand what we're talking about and can respond accordingly (and, fun fact: they don't know the difference between the real experience and the imagined one).

This is why your blood pressure goes up when you're watching an action movie: the lizards are receiving images, and they are triggering your body to protect you. Our subconscious brain will accept our future journey as genuine experiences if we can clearly envision them with details and feelings. The lizards will adjust our subconscious behavior and attitude to be congruent with a new mental image. In short, visualization sends a memo to the lizards, giving them something to work on.

Mental imagery can improve motor control, attention, perception, and memory. Images stimulate the same brain zones and neural connections as actual physical exercise. Unfortunately, this does not mean you can train for the Olympics at home on your sofa. Still, it does mean using these brain connections might help improve our tennis swing.

When we reflect, we use mental imagery to visualize and process the past. But mental imagery is also a tool that allows us to see into the future. It can help us prepare for unexpected circumstances and improve our ability to resist that box of doughnuts. Despite the noble case for getting off our duffs, there are some brilliant and effective practices we can do from the comfort of our chairs, without lifting a finger.

I call these two visualization exercises *snapshots* and *movies*. Snapshots help us see ourselves in the future in static (stationary). Movies help us picture ourselves in dynamic (moving) modes. Here's how that works:

Snapshot: I visualize myself *as a runner* by thinking of myself in a cute jogger outfit.

Movie: I visualize myself *running* by picturing myself jogging down a specific street.

In this sense, *visualization* bridges the gap between the present and the next step.

Steven Covey said, "All things are created twice."[4] He meant that we create things first in our minds and then with our hands and efforts. Allow me to go a step further and say that all things must be created three times: first with words, then with pictures, and then with our hands. Words are the language of the head; images are the language of the HEART (go figure); actions are the language of the hands.

Images are the bridge between thinking and doing.

So is HEART.

How to Visualize Effectively

If you've never intentionally used visualization before (remember, your brain uses it all the time without asking for permission!), you might not know where to start. The basic concept is simple: imagine yourself doing the next step. But to make it stick (and make it effective), try the following strategies:

- Start by visualizing yourself performing this new habit: If someone photographed you in the middle of this activity, what would it look like? Where would you be? What would you be wearing? What would your expression look like?
- Then, add movement: Imagine the movie of yourself in the future, working on a habit or

routine. We won't visualize something way in the future, like the finish line of a marathon. It is not enough to visualize the finish line; we must use vision to prepare for the entire sequence and next steps, whatever they may be: getting up, stretching, and running in the morning.

- Add in details of the surroundings: the weather, the temperature, the lighting, the smells, the textures, the sounds of the environment.
- Anticipate your emotional experience: Will you feel resistance? Will you be tired? Will it feel good to move your body? How will you feel after?
- Anticipate obstacles and how you will respond: You accidentally slept past your alarm. What's your backup plan? It's storming outside. What then? Write the whole narrative if you can. If you keep seeing it in your mind, you won't worry when it occurs. Picture yourself overcoming the factors that would weaken your confidence, derail, or distract you. This reduces the feeling of being in the unknown and therefore reduces stress.
- Repeat: Visualize as much as possible. Practice daily to form a new habit. Until we embrace our new self-image, we won't see transformation. Do this daily.

The most important part of this process is that you start where you are.

You cannot fool yourself; visualizing yourself as a marathon runner when you haven't run a mile in the history of ever will not turn you into a world-class athlete (and you might get hurt). Instead, start where you are.

Visualization, which will move you forward, is based on acceptance: "With my present knowledge and assumptions, what can I achieve?" If you can visualize yourself as a walker and follow through with the action of walking, however small, you will develop trust in yourself and in the new identity you're living into.

The result is a self-image that supports the habits and routines of your HEART. Little by little, we change. We see those changes in the mirror, because we started by satisfying our foundational needs, life became a self-fulfilling prophecy, reinforcing our choices with the reward of balance, and then beauty.

The work of change requires that we acknowledge where we are and keep moving forward. The only way to hold both of those actions simultaneously is to be gracious with ourselves. When we practice self-compassion, we remind ourselves of the truth that everyone starts somewhere. We cultivate the habit of speaking to ourselves gently, saying things like:

I'm doing the best I can.

This is good enough for today.

What do I need right now?

This is difficult. It's okay to go slow.

This was not part of my plan. It's okay to regroup.

I'm doing a good job with what I've been given.

When we can speak to ourselves like a kind friend, we can see where we are and accept it, even when that present reality doesn't match the life we'd hoped for.

After seeing results like that, it's easier to make those counterintuitive choices.

If your sleep improves because you make choices that improve sleep, you'll quit making choices that impede sleep. You'll drink more water as new habits gradually replace old ones. You'll see changes with a nutrition plan in place. You'll move more because you will stop overthinking workouts and start going for walks. Start small and work your way up.

Write It Down, Make It Beautiful

1. List things you like about yourself. Maybe you have great shoulders, a sense of humor, a sympathetic heart. We often apologize for features like these. Take some time to be grateful for them.

2. List skills you possess. Maybe you can cook, make a mean cocktail, entertain children and dogs, or make that funny *Star Trek* hand gesture! Big or small, take a moment to appreciate your gifts and abilities.

3. List things you're proud of. This is my favorite dinner party question. It gives people a chance to tell you what really matters to them, without feeling like they're bragging. So, go on, brag!

4. List hardships you have overcome. What skills helped you overcome? Make note of these characteristics to remind yourself of your strength, spirit, and potential.

5. List people who have helped you. How would these people describe you? What positive traits would they say you have? Note these traits and use visualization to incorporate them into your self-image.

6. List people you have helped. When you help others, you provide value to yourself and to them.

7. List things you appreciate about your life. Go for double digits on this one! Small gratitude brings great change. It could be something as small and temporary as a dish soap bubble, but appreciating it will transform your life.

8. This week, ask yourself this question: Can I see where I'm going? Take that mental picture and go!

Chapter 11

SMALL WINS AND LASTING CHANGE

"You only live once, but if you do
it right, once is enough."
MAE WEST

HEART asks you to make many changes. It is tempting to try to do it all in one stride—in one week or one month.

Rapid growth and swift change work for some people. I've seen it. And sometimes, that quick change sticks.

But this is the exception to the rule. How often do we cancel the gym membership? Revert to old habits after one week? How often do we gain the weight back or make the same relationship mistake?

How Do We Create Lasting Change?

I, for one, put my money on small steps, on little progress. Small steps become practices, and those disciplines begin a chain reaction that brings lasting growth.

Step 1: Start with a Small Step

As you address your needs in the five Life Segments and make progress in each arena, I want to underscore the importance of taking it slow when you need it. Life isn't a race. She who dies with the most progress does not win.

You don't have to go from drinking three cups of coffee, a soda, and wine each day to only drinking water. That's a big change. Instead, try drinking only water for a certain period in the day, say, 10:00 to 3:00 p.m. Or, if getting a walk or workout in seems like an impossible task, don't expect yourself to do it daily. Try two or three times a week.

This is especially important when we are in a tough season. Perhaps getting through the next thirty minutes without bursting into tears is progress. Start there.

If you want to begin a new daily routine, aim for three days in a row instead of thirty. Small action isn't worthless—it's *action*. Just because the experts say habits take twenty-seven, or sixty, or whatever days to become a habit, it doesn't mean my three days are worthless.

For instance, I don't know if I can brush my teeth first thing in the morning every day this month, but I *know* I can brush my teeth every morning for the next three days! I am confident, encouraged, and will now run out to buy new organic toothpaste. Three days from now, I will be elated because I will be a winner! A goal-setter! A habit-tracker! In short, the choice to act— even in the smallest, most minuscule way—brought about the benefits of belief change, which establishes the foundation for all transformation.

Step 2: Celebrate That Small Step

I count the smallest wins. If getting out of bed has been a challenge, and you get out of bed, *celebrate*! I'm not saying grab a glass of bubbly at 8:00 a.m. but pat yourself on the back. Award yourself points for whatever is a big deal to you.

You can be proud of three days of accomplishment. You can be proud of the first time you do something new. You can choose to acknowledge yourself.

The only way to change is to love yourself enough to acknowledge your wins without comparison. The only way to change your life is one tiny step at a time. You say to yourself, I know I can do that. Small wins matter. The celebration cements this new belief in self-change. The more you can imagine your new self and prove you can change, the better.

Step 3: Build on the Small Step

The only way to create lasting change: build on small win after small win. When you're drafting a book, words become sentences, and sentences become paragraphs. One minute of willpower turns into five, then ten, then twenty. A masterpiece is born one brushstroke at a time. Mountains are moved one rock at a time.

When It Feels Anything but Graceful

We all have defense mechanisms. Inadvertent self-sabotage occurs all the time. We have bad habits, and despite our best intentions, those habits can sometimes take over. What do we do when the road to "ride a bike" feels . . . *bumpier* than we imagined?

Recognize Self-Sabotage

Commit to paying attention to yourself. I know this sounds simple on the surface, but the truth is, it's not easy to bring awareness into your life. One technique I use is journaling every day. Journaling helps me tell the truth to myself, even when the truth feels sticky.

What upset you?

What threw you off track?

Did anything make you react?

Then look at what's on the paper: Would you say those things to a friend? Awareness is the first step.

Clarify Your Values

Remind yourself what makes life beautiful: your health, relationships, and ability to enjoy life and participate in what matters to you. Remind yourself of these values in whatever way works for you: lists taped to your mirror or mementos on the fridge. With a clear sense of what matters in life, you will have the courage to overcome the habits that stand in the way.

Identify Non-Sabotaging Alternatives to an Activity

Now that you've identified how your self-sabotage hinders you, it's time to replace that activity with something else. Try swapping stress-eating for a jog. Replace an hour of Netflix with a call with a friend. Make a list of activities you usually procrastinate on and prepare for them instead. Pay close attention to others in similar situations: How does another mom deal with feelings of mom-guilt (if that's what your sabotage protects you from)?

Gather Support

Adopting new behaviors is complicated. Self-sabotage is difficult to overcome without support. When I'm trying to overcome a limiting belief, I'll confide in David or admit it to a close friend who can hold me accountable. They are voices of compassion when I'm at the end of my rope. For others, support may come in the form of delegating tasks, or even waiting on tasks (leaving the vacuuming undone, for example), so that you can focus on your emotional health.

Maybe support means more nature walks or prayer or time alone in a warm bath. Digital communities are another source of support. Whatever you're facing, likely someone else out there can relate. Find your people and allow them to cheer you on.

Adapt to Discomfort

It takes emotional endurance to establish new habits. Because the lizards in the amygdala are freaking out, it will be uncomfortable. Our lizards are there to stay, so we might as well make peace with them. Listen to them. What circumstances or past trauma is triggering them? And then gently reassure them that you've got this. It is tempting to avoid the discomfort by slipping back into old routines. Resist. Keep working toward your values.

Set Boundaries

As you observe yourself, you'll recognize those boxes with trigger warnings on them—the ones that drive the lizards insane. Avoid these until you become comfortable with alternative activities.

- Can you avoid a stressful situation before it happens?
- Can you control when you see a certain person who pushes your buttons?
- Can you set boundaries to help you avoid triggers?

Create a New Inner Voice Track

Journalist and author Elizabeth Gilbert said, "You need to learn how to choose your ideas, just like you select your clothing daily."[1] If you want to have control over your life, focus on your thinking. That should be the *only thing* you attempt to control.

Self-sabotage relies on our critical inner voice. As we become aware of our self-sabotaging tendencies, we will learn how to speak kindly to ourselves.

If you hear classically self-defeating messages like:

- Who do you think you are?
- You could never do that.
- You're such a loser.
- Why do you even try?

Can you give that voice a new track? When you hear yourself think those thoughts, pause, and try out something kind to yourself:

- You are discovering who you are!
- You have so many valuable skills, and you're learning more even now!
- You're doing the best you can.
- You are so brave for trying!

Focus on the possibility instead of probability, the truth of who you are outside of whatever you're facing, and the opportunity for growth.

Give Yourself Grace

Finally, even when your process doesn't feel graceful, you deserve grace. It is your birthright. You don't have to do anything to earn it. You deserve it because you're human, and you're here, and you're absolutely doing your best.

Being hard on yourself about sabotaging behaviors will only keep you from understanding the why. The key is compassion—tons of compassion for yourself as you navigate this journey from your head to your HEART.

What to Do When You Feel Like You're Failing

I'm in the business of helping people organize their lives. But even being in the business of organization doesn't mean I am perfectly organized. Far from it. I regularly feel like a hot mess. There are days I do the opposite of everything I'm advising: I play dumb games on my phone instead of reading, straightening my office, or reading to my kids. But part of figuring out how to meet my needs is having compassion for myself.

With compassion in place, I can safely ask myself why I made those choices, and what I might do differently or better next time. Sometimes this means admitting I need help. And by golly, there is no shame in that. We are all juggling a copious volume of tasks.

I go back to the basics of HEART when I've dropped the ball, either because of my choices, circumstances, or because I generally feel like a failure.

In her book *Dare to Lead*, Brené Brown writes, "I know my life is better when I work from the assumption that everyone is doing the best they can."[2]

It's not a bad thing to drop the ball sometimes. The berating voice beating us up needs to be reminded, "I'm doing the best I can right now."

And when I fall or fail, I remind myself I did the best I could with what I knew and understood at that time. This grace for myself paves the mental road for me to realize I could have done better, without beating myself up. When I fail, compassion gives me the perspective to see what I can do better next time. I'm showing myself compassion while being brutally honest about what went wrong and what I can do differently next time.

Be abundantly gracious with yourself. Consider how this sounds: "[Your Name Here], you really killed this day." Or "Don't worry, [Your Name], you'll provide so much value in that meeting." Or "You look pretty today!" Maybe it's, "Excellent nutrition choice, [Your Name], I'm proud of you." Sometimes, it's, "I know you didn't feel it today, and you know what, that's okay. You did the best you could with the time, energy, and focus you had. Thank goodness, there's always tomorrow. I can't wait to see you then. Now get some shut-eye. It's going to be a big day."

Does talking to yourself in your head feel corny or sound encouraging? I call it a genuine and sincere vote of confidence from someone who believes in me when I don't believe in myself.

Throughout our lives, we all experience different seasons. There are mountaintop moments, when everything feels possible, contrasted with bouts of depression and discouragement that render the smallest tasks impossible. When that happens (and it will), remember that's normal and remind yourself you are doing the best you can. That doesn't mean give up. It means giving yourself the grace you need to get through the season you're in. Loving yourself this way will allow you to ask for what you need. Find support—engage family or friends to discuss what is hard. Find a therapist, a psychiatrist, a medical practitioner, a trainer. Consider medication or therapy, and reach out to your faith community—or take a step toward one, if you don't have one. HEART is founded on the principle that you have needs and must act to meet them.

There are, of course, times when I need to hear hard truths from myself. But that's part of love. Love is a balance of grace and truth.

I must ask myself, "Which do I need to practice today?" For instance, my truth today is, "No, Whitney, you need to go workout." In the words of Eleanor Roosevelt, "You must do the thing you think you cannot do." Truth moment: action required—get on the bike.

But grace moments are equally important. Maybe you're overextended in other areas, and you need a break. An old wound reopened or you're mentally preparing for a major change.

Consider how you would look at a friend and offer grace. Can you offer that to yourself? Is it a truth moment or a grace moment? You must have the self-awareness to know which response is appropriate for the situation.

The real risk is denial. Heads buried, we pretend worst case won't happen, putting our partners, kids, coworkers, clients, or friends at imposition in their own lives. We must be honest with ourselves and our people about our capacity.

Admitting you will drop the ball is the first step to accomplishing that goal in the long run. Tell yourself, "A ball will be dropped today," and then choose the ball. Prioritize your stuff and see what falls off, then communicate with the affected parties. Know that those people will survive.

If the changes disappoint your child, know that you haven't ruined their life forever. They will still graduate from high school.

Lastly, do your best to remind yourself that HEART is a practice, not a terminal destination.

A friend of mine texted me the other day, saying, "I feel like I'm failing at this." "This" being HEART. I told her what I'll tell you: it's impossible to fail at HEART. That's because HEART is a practice, not something you do once and mark complete.

If you miss tennis practice, then you miss tennis practice. You try not to, but it happens. You don't beat yourself up about it. You go back to the courts the next day. Can we apply this same attitude to HEART practices? If you make a goal to eat one salad a day or drink more water and you don't, can you resist the urge to beat yourself up and instead say, "Tomorrow!" Remember, your mindset can be your friend or your enemy here.

No matter who you are or what your situation is, remember your power. My progress has looked different in various seasons. My point is, whatever season you're in, there can be a better one right around the corner if you focus on your needs.

Write It Down, Make It Beautiful

You can look at all these lists and see the impossible, or you can see a challenge. Tell yourself:

1. When you look at all your lists and see the impossible, how can you show yourself some grace?
2. How can you reduce your speed and find a sustainable pace?
3. Brainstorm ideas on how you can recognize and appreciate the small wins.

Chapter 12

HEART IN ACTION

"Yesterday is gone. Tomorrow has not yet come. We have only today. Let us begin."

MOTHER TERESA

When people ask me how I came up with HEART, I usually tell them I didn't come up with it. I *uncovered* it. It feels like something bigger than me, a collective effort between Jesus, a Jewish psychologist, and every person who's ever wanted a better life than the life she has now.

When I set out to rebalance my life, I thought I was creating a new way to set goals. Like so many of you, I aspired to a life I could never quite achieve. Something was always holding me back. Frustrated by my lack of progress and desperate to grasp a life out of reach, I was afraid to hope life might ever be beautiful again.

I don't feel that way anymore.

Remember that terrible day I told you about? The day I found out the business was bankrupt?

For a long time, that memory stung. I'd done everything the way I'd been told and taught and still ended up Mayor of Failure City. The first time I even *considered* setting goals again, I cringed, cried, and tried to find somewhere to hide. Harbored resentment accumulated in my heart, as I watched others achieve goals I had set and tried to achieve. I thought I was angry at my goals, but really I was just angry at anybody who looked like they had a life more beautiful than mine.

There were multiple points of failure, of course. But I felt most betrayed by and disappointed in my goals, ambitions, hopes, and dreams. I questioned everything I had ever hoped for or dreamed about.

What was the point of hoping for a better future, or dreaming big dreams, if no matter how hard I worked, I ended up *here*?

Despite the disappointment in my dreams, a deep internal desire for a better, or at least less chaotic, life remained. I didn't need the best—good or better would suffice. I was tired of trying to be the best only to end up in the most awful, shameful place I could imagine. The longing for something restored, however vague it was, kept me going.

At that juncture, as with all crossroads, I had several choices. I could rage, defiantly refuse to set goals, declaring they just didn't work for me. Or I could take ownership of my story, all the good and bad and gory and glorious parts of it. I could learn as much as possible about myself, understand my wiring and brain and intrinsic motivators, understand how God created me and the vision He wanted for my life, and try this goal-setting thing again, but differently.

I chose the latter.

Doing goals differently meant that I needed a new acronym. Kid you not, I picked HEART because it rhymed with SMART and when you have ambitions to be a thought leader, you think literary devices like that are cool.

My first year using HEART helped me to set more balanced goals. Still ambitious, I chose three goals for each Life Segment, and even allowed myself three wild card goals. Eighteen goals in total. While still a little overzealous, my willingness to make mistakes had several benefits. Instead of being hyper-focused on one area, all areas of my life saw growth and improvement. Nothing was neglected. Little by little, changes started to add up.

About halfway through that year, I had a light-bulb moment: eighteen goals were unnecessary, unrealistic, and far too many. One goal in each of the Life Segments would be more than enough, and I didn't need more than five goals in total.

The second year I used HEART to set my goals, I stumbled across an article about Maslow. I remembered back to my college psych class; he was the needs guy. As I read the article, I realized the Life Segments paralleled well with our primary human needs. This was the moment when the order of the Life Segments fell into place. Just as Maslow identified that needs are satisfied in a certain order, the idea that the order of our priorities can contribute to the success or failure of our goals solidified.

This generated a shift in my approach to goal organization. What if we looked at goals through the lens of human need, instead of rooting our goals in human desires? The starting question changed from "What do you want?" to "What do you *need*?" When I structured my goals around my needs, everything changed.

It was like putting on magic glasses that make everything look rosy—like heaven. The burdens of "I am supposed to do this" and "I *should* do that" lifted. My language evolved: instead of saying can't, I said maybe, possibly, likely. As I had more compassion for myself, the way I saw others changed too. It's easier to love difficult people if you're trying to understand them.

The third year, I didn't use HEART to set my goals, because I didn't set goals. In lieu of *annual* goals, I used HEART to focus on my monthly and weekly *needs* instead.

As I focused my attention on one need at a time, prioritizing the seemingly small needs (health, relationships, home) over the big projects (work), life started looking up. Actually, it started looking a lot like a life designed for me, instead of one I'd drawn out of a hat at the goals seminar. I rather liked it.

The amazing thing about a life that's in balance is that you feel much more open to the hopes and dreams you have stuffed to the bottom of your heart, like seeds buried under the compost of mistakes and missteps. Braver and quieter than I had been about my goals, I asked myself, *How can HEART help me reach my potential?*

Slowly but surely, it *worked*. I don't mean I achieved my potential. Focusing on the Life Segments, life balanced out, and then even the *big things* fell into place. Big dreams I'd been dreaming for years—but unable to make happen—began just . . . happening. Inexplicably. My fledgling business took off, our marriage got stronger, and my overall health improved.

I'll be honest: the narrow focus on the five Life Segments made things feel sluggish at first—a pace I'm not accustomed to. But that's because we're used to Amazon Prime speed, and the good stuff of life can't be ordered online and delivered overnight. Growth takes time.

It worked, and it worked beautifully.

In fact, it worked so well that the idea of setting goals faded into the background. Now HEART became the way I filtered my entire life.

- The H became daily: If I want to lose five pounds, the daily activity is eat a salad every day.
- The E became daily: If I want to read more books, the daily activity required is ten pages.
- The A became daily and weekly: Better relationships with my people mean one meaningful conversation with each of them, daily, or checking in on them weekly.
- The R became weekly and monthly: Maintaining my car starts with cleaning out trash when I get gas. My prep day set me up for a great week.
- I'll be honest about *Trade and Talent*. It's a Life Segment laden with projects—and it's the hardest to manage. But as I used the other four Life Segments to prioritize my days, I found more time, and better time, and a heart overflowing to invest in managing my projects.

So to recap . . .

After one year of HEART. *Life was steady and balanced. Nice. Good, even.* I hadn't made a million dollars, bought a private jet, run a marathon, or lost twenty pounds. Still, I had great relationships with David and our kids. We were cooking healthy meals at home, my weight wasn't ballooning, the kitchen was staying (relatively) clean. Work was working—probably because I wasn't measuring it by the daily bank account balance or obsessing over long-term projections.

After two years of HEART. *I felt slow, steady growth coming to my life.* We were walking more, the weight I'd long been trying to lose was starting to come off, our family was close—the stuff that *mattered* was happening. Conversations with our kids about stewardship and school and choices were happening. Thoughtful decisions about finances were happening. Using HEART every day, instead of just annually, had helped our family create a sustainable cadence.

After three years of HEART. *The ambitions and goals I'd been so nervous to embrace showed up again.* Not because I forced them. Not because I arbitrarily made them by comparing my life to someone who I liked more than I liked me. But they started coming from a deep, steady, balanced, beautiful place called my own heart. I wasn't shouting from the rooftops or on Instagram about them. The process was, at times, messy. But things felt good and right. My progress toward them was slow but sure, the way you grow a baby in your belly or an oak tree in your backyard.

I'm not afraid of myself anymore. I'm not afraid to admit I have flaws, am in process, and learning as I go. I'm not running or rushing or hiding or seeking or worrying or freaking out. And I love the pace of a peaceful life, even if it does mean I might drive like a little old lady now.

Of course, the chaos still finds its way into our lives. Months into a very chaotic 2020, David and I realized we would need to make a move. It wasn't planned—nothing about 2020 was planned, amiright? But after a series of events, it became obvious we were supposed to at least *look* for a new home.

A long time ago, David and I developed a policy. If we have to make a big decision, and are unsure what the right choice is, we "push against the door to see if it opens." In other words, if you're standing in a hallway with a bunch of closed doors, each door being a possible option, we walk around and rattle the doorknobs to see which are unlocked.

In this instance, we started looking at houses. We looked for one and a half days and then walked into a house *perfect* for us. It was four doors down from my parents, in our price range, and a total fixer upper. Designed by an architect in the sixties, it featured cedar details, wood floors, and enough garage space for me to have a studio.

When we took the kids to see it for the first time, I told them I wanted to see what God had done as we walked into the backyard. Over the past few years, David and I had continued to unravel the consequences of choices that hadn't led us to where God had wanted us to be. We'd done this by living in rented houses, too small houses, wrong location houses, and my kids had always mourned the absence of a *real* backyard.

But when I walked them into this backyard, I didn't need to use any words. All three of them burst into a run, screaming and celebrating the part of the house I knew they would love the most: space to be kids. To run, to laugh, to play.

I think that's what heaven will feel like. When we are sitting on the front porches of our mansions (I'll take 900 square feet, if I'm in charge of cleaning it, thanks, Lord), we'll look back on our lives and see how the times we made the tough choices led us to that point. We'll see how everything hard in this life ends up making sense.

This world makes it difficult to slow down and be satisfied with little (or much, as I recently said to a friend that *does* have a private plane). It's easy to be frustrated with my discontent—with where I am, how fast I am going, who is winning. But magic (aka confidence) happens when we shift our perspective:

- From what do I want to what do I need
- From who I am today to who I am becoming
- From where I want to be to where I am
- From my dreams to an inspired vision for my life
- From outcome to process
- From destination to journey
- From not knowing my limits to listening to my capacity
- From planning to doing
- From doing all the things to doing one thing at a time
- From celebrating big wins to celebrating daily

My journey through goal-setting to HEART changed the way I think about goals. I still have ambitions, dreams, and hopes, but I don't focus on them. I have goals, but I don't set them, fix them in concrete, and never let them change—a win/lose, pass or fail test of my potential.

I've learned (the hard way) that my best work will not happen if I'm tired or sick, emotionally unhealthy, don't have great relationship support, or if my finances are falling apart. Keeping everything under control doesn't take much effort, if I do it first, daily.

Balance, turns out, rides most smoothly between success and failure.

In trying to reinvent the way I achieved my dreams, I found something more important: my everyday, beautiful life. I found my HEART.

Your Life with HEART

Setting goals this new way changed me.

If you embrace HEART, your life will change too.

I suggest using HEART every day at first. Post the twelve checkpoints on your bathroom mirror or in your bedroom. Review it before you go to sleep. Visualize making one bit of progress on each letter as you go to sleep. Then tackle it in the morning. Make small progress on each checkpoint. Go in order.

In time, it won't be necessary to refer to it every day. Your habits will take over. But it's still helpful for planning. Use HEART to plan your week, month, and year. Compare it with your calendar to make sure you're taking care of you.

At this point, you can return to HEART and you're back on track. When you have an off day, something feels off-kilter, that's when it's time to take a moment, take a breath, and review your list.

There are many ways a day gets derailed. Some of my derailed days have included waking up to kids fighting, sick kids, or kids who have just informed me they forgot to finish a project due that day. If someone is sick, has an early appointment, or has forgotten to tell me about an important detail of the day, my morning routine is hijacked. These days, I adore HEART even more than usual, because HEART makes regaining control so much easier.

The first sign of a day derailed isn't what's happening around me, it's how I feel. If I'm frustrated because of a messy kitchen or fighting kids, I've learned to recognize the frustration as anxiety—a warning flag. While my first instinct is to break up the fighting kids, or start washing dishes, those are just symptoms of a deeper issue: I'm not managing myself well. Practices from *Help Yourself* and *Empower Yourself* are helpful here:

- Did I get enough sleep the night before? If I didn't, I give myself grace and remind myself to go to bed early that night. The reward of a good night's sleep is sometimes the only motivation I need to get through the day—and I take the day as easy as possible, conserving my emotional and physical energy. On these days, focusing on managing my energy is essential.

- Am I drinking enough water? My mom tells me to drink a glass of water when I'm tired. She's been around longer than I have, so I consider this good advice. It's also simple and easy to do and builds momentum toward a more productive and satisfying day.

- How's my nutrition? Less sugar, more salads. If I'm feeling sluggish or frustrated with circumstances, healthy food choices empower me to feel more in control of my day and build momentum.

- Am I moving? Walking is some of the best mental, emotional, and physical work we can do for ourselves. Parking far away from the store or walking to the store while running errands is a great way to squeeze my walks in. If David and I need to talk, we've found walking is a great way to get away from the kids and have a conversation. We'll make them run ahead while we take it a bit more slowly. Sometimes, I'll take the stairs, to get some extra movement in. I don't focus on how many steps I've taken; I focus on taking advantage of the right opportunities to move.

- How's my emotional state? Therapy is expensive; journaling is free (though I still think therapy's worth the cost if you can afford it). Whether journaling or processing with a therapist, I'm trying to get to know my *inner world* a little bit better. Instead of blaming other people and events for "making me" feel something, I've found it more empowering to take ownership of my feelings. I acknowledge the emotion and admit to myself I am choosing to feel this way. No one and nothing can make me feel anything unless I give them permission. It's a bonus if I have the time to journal about it. Reminding myself to take responsibility and make a different choice is often the most effective step to get my day back on track. Taking ownership improves patience with my kids, because it gives me pause. I contribute to the predicament when I snap; I contribute to the solution when I coach them to process their disagreements and hold them to a higher standard.

- Have I renewed my mind? We must be intentional about feeding our thoughts. This might mean it's time to turn off the news or the true crime podcast and listen to something more uplifting, or even read some fiction.

- How's my soul? Most of us believe we are spiritual beings created by a higher power. Ignoring our soul is ignoring our purpose. When I neglect this part of myself, I neglect my potential, gifts, talents, and strengths. If my day is feeling derailed by this, the warning sign is extreme frustration. I'm ignoring my spirit when I muscle through challenges on my own strength or attempt to solve problems without inviting God or His guidance. Taking care of my soul usually means going "palms up," as Bob Goff has taught me— holding the outcome loosely, and mentally choosing to trust what needs to happen will happen.[1]

Very often, if a day has gone off the rails, it's for one of those seven reasons.

After H and E, I usually proceed down the acronym. But not always. Making it all the way through the acronym isn't the point. HEART isn't another chore to chop off your already-insane checklist. This is your chance to check in with yourself. It's a way for you to nourish yourself so you can be more balanced. It's a way for you to steady yourself so you can see how beautiful your life already is.

The Grace to Live in the Present

The biggest change I've seen in my own life—and my hope for you—is the introduction of grace into my life. I no longer see myself as behind or beat myself up for not being Superwoman. I don't shame myself, or when I do, it's only for a moment. Then I remind myself I'm doing the best I can. I show up for myself and, because of that, I show up for other people. I find joy in doing the dishes, riding bikes with the kids, waiting in line, reading a book. There's beauty in everything, if only we stop to notice it: a crazy, messy, beautiful life.

Write It Down, Make It Beautiful

1. What does a beautiful life look like for you? With your needs met, what type of person are you empowered to be?
2. Make a list of adjectives or phrases describing the beautiful person you're becoming and the beautiful life you're living now. Print it out or make a collage, and put it somewhere you can see it.

NOTES

Introduction

1. Alain de Botton, *The Architecture of Happiness* (UK: Penguin Book LTD, 2014).
2. Eric Schulzke, "You'd Think Cursive Doesn't Matter Anymore, but It Does," *Deseret News*, June 5, 2014, https://www.deseret.com/2014/6/5/20542619/ you-d-think-cursive-doesn-t-matter-anymore-but-it-does.

Chapter 1: Goals Gone Wrong

1. Francine Jay, *Miss Minimalist: Inspiration to Downsize, Declutter, and Simplify* (Anja Press, 2011), Kindle.
2. "Q. Where can I find information on Yale's 1953 goal study?" Yale University Library, answered September 28, 2020, https://ask.library.yale.edu/faq/175224.
3. Alina Dizik, "Why Your New Year's Resolutions Often Fail," BBC, December 25, 2016, https:// www.bbc.com/worklife/article/20161220-why-your-new-years-resolutions-often-fail.
4. Andy Stanley, *Visioneering* (New York: Crown Publishing Group, 2012).
5. Stanley, *Visioneering*.
6. Steve Kamb, "The Cautionary Tale of South Park's Underpants Gnomes," Observer, January 12, 2016, https://observer.com/2016/01/the-cautionary-tale-of-south-parks-underpants-gnomes.

7. Geoffrey James, "What Goal-Setting Does to Your Brain and Why It's Spectacularly Effective," Inc., October 23, 2019, https://www.inc.com/kimberly-weisul/shearshare-tye-caldwell-studying -relationships-kindergarten-paying-off.html.

Chapter 2: HEART Explained

1. J. K. Rowling, *Very Good Lives: Fringe Benefits of Failure and the Importance of Imagination* (UK: Sphere Books, 2015).
2. Dr. Saul McLeod, "Maslow's Heirarchy of Needs," *Simply Psychology*, December 29, 2020, https:// www.simplypsychology.org/maslow.html.

Chapter 3: "It's Like Riding a Bike!"

1. "Sabotage," Merriam-Webster, accessed November 4, 2021, https://www.merriam-webster.com /dictionary/sabotage.
2. Christina R. Wilson, "What Is Self-Sabotage? How to Help Stop the Vicious Cycle," Positive Psychology, August 17, 2021, https://positivepsychology.com/self-sabotage/.
3. Robert W. Firestone, Lisa Firestone, Joyce Catlett, and Pat Love, *Conquer Your Critical Inner Voice: A Revolutionary Program to Counter Negative Thoughts and Live Free from Imagined Limitations* (Oakland: New Harbinger Publications, 2002).
4. Elyssa Barbash, PhD, "Different Types of Trauma: Small 't' versus Large 'T,'" *Psychology Today*, March 13, 2017, https://www.psychologytoday.com/us/blog/trauma-and-hope/201703/different -types-trauma-small-t-versus-large-t.
5. Eva M. Krockow, PhD, "How Many Decisions Do We Make Each Day?" *Psychology Today*, September 27, 2018, https://www.psychologytoday.com/us/blog/stretching-theory/201809 /how-many-decisions-do-we-make-each-day.
6. Amy Marschall, "The Four Fear Responses: Fight, Flight, Freeze, and Fawn," Verywell Mind, October 26, 2021, https://www.verywellmind.com/the-four-fear-responses-fight-flight-freeze -and-fawn-5205083.

Chapter 4: H–Help Yourself

1. Jane Austen, *Mansfield Park* (UK: Thomas Egerton, 1814).
2. Luciana Besedovsky, Tanja Lange, and Jan Born, "Sleep and Immune Function," *Pflugers Archiv: European Journal of Physiology* 463, 1 (2012): 121–37, published online November 10, 2011,

https://link.springer.com/article/10.1007/s00424-011-1044-0?correlationId=ac0e3b7c-03d9-47d0-8ac6-cce856c91e8f.

3. "Sharpen Thinking Skills with a Better Night's Sleep," Harvard Health Publishing: Harvard Medical School, March 1, 2014, https://www.health.harvard.edu/mind-and-mood/sharpen-thinking-skills-with-a-better-nights-sleep.

4. Mark R. Rosekind et al., "The Cost of Poor Sleep: Workplace Productivity Loss and Associated Costs," *Journal of Occupational and Environmental Medicine* 52, 1 (January 2010): 91–98, https://pubmed.ncbi.nlm.nih.gov/20042880/.

5. "High Blood Pressure: How Does Sleep Affect Your Heart Health?" Center for Disease Control and Prevention, accessed November 7, 2021, https://www.cdc.gov/bloodpressure/sleep.htm.

6. "High Blood Pressure: How Does Sleep Affect Your Heart Health?"

7. Jon Johnson, "How to Tell If Stress Is Affecting Your Sleep," Medical News Today, September 5, 2018, https://www.medicalnewstoday.com/articles/322994.

8. Alanna Morris et al., "Sleep Quality and Duration Are Associated with Higher Levels of Inflammatory Biomarkers: The META-Health Study," *Circulation* 122, S21 (November 2010): Abstract 17806, https://www.ahajournals.org/doi/10.1161/circ.122.suppl_21.A17806.

9. "High Blood Pressure: How Does Sleep Affect Your Heart Health?"

10. "High Blood Pressure: How Does Sleep Affect Your Heart Health?"

11. Jeana Medlin, "How Does Hydration Affect Bone Density and Health, Sport Ortho Urgent Care Center?" accessed November 7, 2021, https://sportorthourgentcare.com/how-does-hydration-affect-bone-density-health/.

12. "Water: Essential to Your Body," Mayo Clinic, July 22, 2020, https://www.mayoclinichealthsystem.org/hometown-health/speaking-of-health/water-essential-to-your-body.

13. "6 Benefits of Drinking Water," Johnston UNC Health Care, February 18, 2019, https://www.johnstonhealth.org/fitness-health/health-matters-blog/fitness-nutrition/2019/benefits-drinking-water/.

14. "Improve Your Mood—Stay Hydrated!" Massachusetts Department of Public Health, August 1, 2017, https://blog.mass.gov/publichealth/mental-wellness/improve-your-mood-stay-hydrated/.

15. "How Does Exercise Reduce Stress? Surprising Answers to This Question and More," Harvard Health Publishing: Harvard Medical School, July 7, 2020, https://www.health.harvard.edu/staying-healthy/exercising-to-relax.

16. "How Does Exercise Reduce Stress?"

17. "Big Rocks–Stephen R. Covey," Franklin Covey, accessed November 7, 2021, https://resources.franklincovey.com/the-8th-habit/big-rocks-stephen-r-covey.

Chapter 6: A–All Your People

1. "75-Year Harvard Study: What Makes Us Happy?" AP News, April 21, 2019, https://apnews.com/article/6dab1e79c34e4514af8d184d951f5733.

Chapter 7: R–Resources and Responsibilities

1. Sofia Alvim, "The Real Definition of Clutter," Huffpost, December 6, 2017, https://www.huffpost.com/entry/the-real-definition-of-clutter_b_9791568.

Chapter 8: T–Trade and Talent

1. Frederick Buechner, *Wishful Thinking: A Theological ABC* (New York: HarperOne, 1993).

Chapter 9: The Power of Your HEART

1. "Routine Is a Sign of Ambition," Antecedent Ventures, accessed November 14, 2021, https://www.antecedent.vc/single-post/2016/08/04/routine-is-a-sign-of-ambition.
2. James Clear, *Atomic Habits* (New York: Avery, 2018), 74.
3. Charles Duhigg, *The Power of Habit: Why We Do What We Do in Life and Business* (New York: Random House Trade Paperbacks, 2014), 100.

Chapter 10: Is This Thing Broken?

1. "Introduction to CBT," Beck Institute, accessed November 14, 2021, https://beckinstitute.org/about/intro-to-cbt/.
2. Viktor E. Frankl, *Man's Search for Meaning* (Boston: Beacon Press, 2006).
3. Narineh Hartoonian, "The Power of Visualization: Imagining Yourself Doing Something Helps You Achieve Your Goal," Rowan Center for Behavioral Medicine, January 6, 2020, https://www.rowancenterla.com/new-blog/2019-12-20-the-power-of-visualization-imagining-yourself-doing-something-helps-you-achieve-your-goal-cw65h.
4. Shlomo Sprung, "RIP Stephen Covey: Here Are His Famous '7 Habits of Highly Effective People,'" Insider, July 16, 2012, https://www.businessinsider.com/stephen-coveys-7-habits-of-highly-effective-people-2012-7.

Chapter 11: Small Wins and Lasting Change

1. Elizabeth Gilbert, *Eat, Pray, Love: One Woman's Search for Everything Across Italy, India, and Indonesia* (New York: Riverhead Books, 2007).
2. Brené Brown, *Dare to Lead* (New York: Random House, 2018).

Chapter 12: HEART in Action

1. Bob Goff, "Living Palms Up," Faith Gateway, April 30, 2017, https://www.faithgateway.com/love-does-means-living-palms-up/#.YZHpS2DMJPY.

ABOUT THE AUTHOR

Whitney English believes that anyone can live a beautiful life. She believes that gratitude is the birthplace of joy, that people matter, that love is the answer, that if you're real you can't be ugly, that everyone is creative and some of us have just forgotten, and that it's worth trying to be a better version of yourself today than you were yesterday. If you're more into technical details, she's boot-strapped two businesses to seven figures, has a degree in interior design, studied management at Parsons in New York City, and has had her work featured in *O* magazine, the *Wall Street Journal*, and on the *Today Show* (twice). She was featured as one of *Country Living* magazine's Women Entrepreneurs in 2008. One of her favorite dreams-come-true, though, is her husband, David, and their three children. She nightly dreams of a perfectly organized office.